SPARKS FROM THE SMIDDY

The Life of a World Champion Farrier

SPARKS FROM THE SMIDDY

The Life of a World Champion Farrier

David Wilson BEM, FWCF

As told to Andrew Arbuckle

Old Pond
PUBLISHING

First published 2015

Published by
5M Publishing Ltd
Benchmark House
8 Smithy Wood Drive
Sheffield S35 1QN, UK
Tel: +44 (0) 1234 81 81 80
www.5mpublishing.com

A Catalogue record for this book is available from the British Library

ISBN 978-1-910456-05-7

Book layout by Forewords, Oxford
Printed in India by Replika Press Pvt. Ltd.
Photos by David Wilson

Contents

Preface

ABOUT five years ago, my brother asked me if I would give a talk at his Probus Club. My answer was, 'What, me?' His reply was, 'You can do that. Talk about your life as a farrier and blacksmith.' So I told them about my fifty years in the farrier industry.

A friend of mine, Andrew Arbuckle, spoke to me one day while the talk was being discussed and he suggested I should write a book. There and then the seeds were sown.

This is my life story, from an early age when I annoyed my father by nailing horseshoes to the smiddy floor, to winning the World Championship in Calgary, Canada, which then opened the doors to the rest of the world.

It also tells of the start of my working life with my father and my introduction to farrier competitions by Jock McKenzie.

I hope the book explains to my children why, on the third week in June each year, their father would disappear to the Highland Show.

Writing this book has certainly brought back a lot of memories. Memories of schoolboy days, time spent fishing, as well as the good fun and camaraderie enjoyed in competing. Never was there a truer saying than 'it is not the winning but taking part that counts', but I would add that winning is pretty special.

I remember the first time I returned from a competition proudly bearing a red winning ticket and my Mum saying, 'You were lucky today, son.' I replied, 'It was skill, Mum, not luck!'

Dedications

M Y thanks go to my wife Mairi for all her help over the last fifty-seven years. For her typing skills and being able to understand and make sense of my handwriting. Also for the almost impossible job of keeping my nose to the grindstone when the sun was shining and I should have been writing.

To the family, Margaret, Ann, Donna and David for holding the fort when I was away in different parts of the world.

To our grandchildren and great grandchildren, this is part of your family history.

To Jock McKenzie for all his help over the years and for passing on all his knowledge and skills.

To Dad and my forebears for passing on all the genes.

To Colin MacConnachie for the artwork.

And last, but certainly not least, to Andrew Arbuckle, whose idea it was to write this book, his encouragement that kept me going when I wondered what to do next, and his expertise on how to lay out the chapters.

Chapter 1

Winning the World Championship

IT was far from being an original thought, but as I stepped up to the podium to collect the trophy awarded to the World Champion Blacksmith 1985, I wished my father had been able to witness the occasion.

I also wished that by some divine intervention, my father could have been accompanied by my grandfather, my great grandfather, my great, great grandfather and even further back to my three- and four-times great grandfathers.

Why the desire for this gathering of the Wilson family? Simply, all five previous generations of my family were blacksmiths. They had all sweated over their forges. They had then hammered the white-hot metal into shape, then fitted it to horses' hooves; back bent with the horse's leg held between their own legs, they nailed the shoes onto the horn of the hoof.

When their work was completed, they might have exchanged the local gossip with the various grooms and ploughmen who had brought their charges along for new footwear. My ancestors' satisfaction would be gauged by the silver in their pocket for the work and by the clip-clop sound of the new shoes on the village and farm roads as the horses returned back home.

Although they never competed to demonstrate their blacksmith skills, I am sure they would have appreciated my victory. Quite apart from any family pride, my forefathers would have appreciated a pair of well-made horseshoes; a pair judged the best in the world.

As I looked around, the sun was high in the clear blue Calgary sky and even if I was thousands of miles from my home in Fife, I could see a solitary Scottish saltire being waved in the packed grandstands. At various times in my life, I have stood in large crowds watching some sporting match or entertainment, but here the scene had changed and there were more than 70,000 people in the stands watching me and cheering as I received the trophy marking me as a world champion.

For the official presentation, I left behind my working gear and in order to ensure the crowds would know my home country was Scotland, I donned my kilt with its distinctive Wilson tartan. What I had not reckoned on was the announcer's voice with its Canadian

Receiving the world championship trophy from the chairman
of the stampede on the main stage in Calgary.

twang ringing round the stadium. 'The 1985 World Champion Farrier
is David Wilson from Scotland.' A lump came to my throat.

When the announcer came up to me with his microphone and
asked for my thoughts on the victory, I should have said that this
was the culmination of years of hard work and months of specialised
training along with a well-organised plan to win the top award in the
farriery world.

But what I am told I did was thank all those who had supported me
over the years and helped me onto the top step on the podium, with
special mention of my wife, Mairi, and our family. The only trouble
being, I heard later, that my response was in my Scottish tongue, so
that a fair amount of my little speech was not understood by the largely
Canadian audience. One of the few in the audience who understood
what I had been saying caught my arm as I left the stadium, and in
a broad Fife accent said, 'Well done.' She added that she had left
Scotland thirty years ago and had lived in Calgary ever since. She had
left her homeland but her Fife twang had not left her.

It was only after the award ceremony that I, along with many of the
other competitors, relaxed, with time to think back to the four days

of competition. I had competed three years previously at Calgary and the knowledge gained on that visit had proven invaluable.

On my first visit, back in 1982, I had underestimated the effects of the high altitude and found myself short of breath and energy, leaving me in danger of cramping up as I worked against the clock making the shoes. Unlike top athletes who now train at altitude for big competitions in order to get increased oxygen-carrying red-blood corpuscles, all my training was carried out at my own blacksmith's business in Balmullo, and that is less than one hundred feet above sea level.

I also knew from that previous visit that the temperature in the competition tent could rise to over a hundred degrees Fahrenheit with more than a dozen forges belching out flames, adding considerably to the body heat of the one thousand or so spectators crammed in to see the competition.

My solution was to make sure I had plenty of salt in my diet and also to have isotonic drinks to hand throughout the competition. Other competitors were not so prepared and afterwards there was talk of so and so cramping up and being unable to complete the competition.

The first visit to the world championships also raised my awareness of some of the tricks other competitors could get up to. These included letting the new man (me) take the lead, thus allowing the others to follow, picking up where there might be problems such as I encountered with the all-important but temperamental forges. If I had been wise to that sort of game, I might even have won the

Thanking everyone in my Scottish accent after receiving the trophy.

championship on my debut, but I have never lived my life on a 'what if' basis. As it was, I was reserve champion on my first visit and this gave me the resolve to return in 1985 and climb to the top of the podium.

The first visit to Calgary was also helpful as Mairi and I decided we wanted to stay in a quiet part of the city, which like all major centres of population always has a background of noise. Not the sort of preparation needed for a world championship competition, or any contest, come to think of it.

Our hostess, Florence, was the cousin of our friends from Balmullo with whom we had travelled to Calgary on our first visit. Her father had been a blacksmith in Orkney before emigrating to Canada, and her son, John, supplied the horses for the shoeing competition.

She was just like a mother to us. Mairi and I loved her to bits. John was in the film industry and on many occasions he had had to supply hundreds of horses for films. All in all, their home was an ideal place to relax while still concentrating on what would lie ahead.

The competition was run over four days, and while I knew the layout from my previous visit, it was new to Jim Ferrie, with whom I was competing in the two-man competition. He worked as a blacksmith in Ayrshire and we had trained together specially for the pairs competition at Calgary.

The day before the competition was due to start, we went down to the showground to have a look around and let Jim see where we would be working. There we learned the competitors would be split into four rounds per class and that we would not be working at the same time. This would enable us to watch the opposition at work.

The competition was to start with an 'eagle eye' contest, which commenced at 7.00 am. The night before, it seemed days since we had left home and sleep came easily for us. We had to set an early alarm.

The eagle-eye competition is used as a warm up, and it allows the competitors to get used to the fires and anvils. The competitor gets to look at a horse's foot for a mere ten seconds then he is allowed fifteen minutes to make a shoe to fit. The shoe is judged on fit alone with the judges trying the shoe on the foot of the horse. If it is not near the shape, it gets thrown in the scrap bucket, and Mairi, who was in the stand beside the judges, could not believe mine had landed in the scrap heap. No prizes for that one.

That night also saw the start of the forging classes. This is where the competition began to get serious. In each class there were two shoes to make as per the schedule that we had all been notified about months ago when our entries were first accepted.

Although Jim and I had practised making the shoes at home, we found that the steel used in Canada was a different specification from the normal steel we used at home. The Canadian steel was measured in the old imperial standard while we had been used to working with metric-cut metal. I believe you should always expect complications and hurdles in any competition. The only problem is that you do not know where or when they will pop up. However, the different measurement was not fatal as we soon adjusted back to the imperial standard, which was what we had both used as apprentices decades earlier.

On the same evening, after the challenge competition was finished, we had one of the two-man team rounds. For that, we had to make a pair of front draught horseshoes. Jim and I came third in that one and the championship points were starting to build up.

The next day was the live shoeing. The horse I was allocated was quiet and had good feet. Things went well and I finished second. There was another forging class in the evening, where we had to make one hunter shoe and a shoe of the judges' choice. The judges' shoe was shown to us before the class started and we then had to work out how to make it.

As the week progressed, I felt that my work had been improving all the time and I was really pleased when it was announced that I had won that class. I was now one point ahead on the leader board, with one class left to do on the last day.

When we went home to Florence's house that night I kept thinking, 'Now I could win the world championships tomorrow. It's within my reach.' But then I also had to keep adding, 'Just keep calm.' I knew that if I kept the head, as they say in Scotland, and did my normal work, I could make it happen.

The final morning saw me up bright and early and I hurried down to the show ground. Initially there had been more than sixty of the top farriers from fourteen countries scattered across the world competing, but as the competition wore on, their numbers dwindled. By the last day it was down to Shane Carter, an American, and me.

We had not competed against each other before but I knew he had a top reputation and I would have to be on my best form to beat him. In my early days, I had been a fair athlete, winning cups and trophies at the local Highland Games. In these events you knew exactly where the opposition was and what you had to do to win. In farrier competitions, it is very much a case of 'head down and do your best' and when the quality of your work is judged, you hope the judges see it as superior to the opposition. In Calgary at the world championships, the organisers draw from a pool of judges with

Making the judges' choice shoe. Going well.

representatives from different countries, and they can usually iron out the small differences in shoemaking that exist.

The last class was a two-man hind draught horse, where we had to make a pair of heavy shoes out of bars of steel eighteen inches long by one and a quarter inches wide and a half inch in depth. This was one of my favourite shoes, so I felt I would be in with a chance. Jim and I got started and were going well when the fire stopped working. They brought us another forge and gave us time to heat the steel again. Five minutes later, the same thing happened, with the fire going out. This went on four times before we finished. I think because of my experience, I did not panic and probably used the delays to our advantage.

Although I have always been able to concentrate on the job in hand, competing in the world championships brought additional pressures. Nowadays the top competitions have announcers to talk through the competition. This helps the spectators understand what is going on, which is good. However, despite concentrating as hard as I could on hammering out the shoes, I could hear the commentator working up the crowd with the call, 'Let's hear it for the Scotsman,' followed by a roar from the audience.

I might have brought a little of this pressure on myself, as I had made sure my forge had a board stating 'David Wilson Scotland', and for good measure, just before I left home, a friend had presented me with a 'Wilson' head band. It did not matter that its original purpose was to advertise golf clubs, as far as I was concerned. Apart from keeping the sweat out of my eyes in the heat of the competition the head band identified me as Wilson.

He may not have meant to be, but the announcer was very helpful in keeping the competitors fully informed of the time. His priority might have been to wind up the crowd with his shouts of, 'Only five minutes to go,' and then in a voice pitched even higher, 'Only two minutes to go,' but this saved valuable seconds looking at my watch.

Soon, with his voice reaching a crescendo, he was counting down the last ten seconds. Regardless of whether they were finished or not, all the competitors knew that the second the bell went they had to throw their shoes on the ground. There was no leeway for one last hammer blow just to get the shoe spot on. There was no time to sort a nail hole that might not have been quite right. There was no extra time at all.

It was an abrupt finish and the attention moved to the judges. Their deliberations would decide who would be champion. As in all

Standing proud (2nd right) after winning the forging
class, surrounded by an elite band of farriers.

Jim Ferrie (right) and myself (left) with the two-man
draught award received from Ollie Mustad.

competitions where the final product is judged, a degree of subjectivity comes into the equation. Over the years I have competed, there have been times where I quietly disagreed with the judge. That's life. We competitors watched the judges picking up and scrutinising our work. I was quietly confident as I could only remember three occasions in fifty years of competitions where I felt I had turned out better shoes.

The results were read out in reverse order and when our names had not been read out by the time the second placer was announced, I think we knew we had won, but when he said the winners of the two-man competition were Jim Ferrie and David Wilson and the overall 1985 World Champion was David Wilson, Scotland, I think it has to be one of my proudest moments. My intuition had turned into reality, but until the announcement was made, there was no official prior indication I had won the world championship. There were congratulations all round from competitors and spectators who stayed for the last competition.

The world championship trophy is a hand-carved bronze figure of a farrier standing at the anvil with his tools. There are only seven of these in existence. The sponsors are given one, the stampede gets one and the trophy is competed for five years in a row, and then seven new trophies are made and the process starts again.

Earlier in the week, there had been a fun competition where I had won a bottle of excellent cognac. This proved to be a very useful prize, as the evening finished with a big party in the show ground.

It had been a tremendous week, filled with nerves, tension, excitement, disappointments and then the thrill of winning. A week to remember. I was a world champion and a very proud one. The win totally changed my life, opening up doors all around the world.

Chapter 2

The Start of the Wilson Era

TODAY, Kilmany is a sleepy little hamlet just off the main Dundee to Kirkcaldy road. The primary school in the village has long since closed and the church is only opened on occasional Sundays. Most of the residents commute to Dundee or further afield as there is little local employment.

Two centuries ago, visitors came to Kilmany from far and wide to hear Scotland's leading theologian, Thomas Chalmers, expound radical views on the Gospels. Local reports of the time tell of people crossing the river Tay from Dundee in small boats and then walking the five miles to Kilmany to hear his sermons before making the lengthy return journey.

Such were Chalmers' qualities and early promise that he qualified as a minister while only aged nineteen, after seven years of study at St Andrew's University. Chalmers, who went on to found the Free Church in Scotland, would lecture in St Andrew's during the week, ride home to Kilmany on Saturday mornings and do the return eight-mile journey on his horse on Monday morning.

It is possible that on one of those trips to St Andrew's, he passed a young blacksmith, George Wilson, along with his new wife, Betsy, heading towards Kilmany, where George became the village blacksmith in 1813. All his worldly goods were on the horse and cart that, I assume, he hired from one of the local farms.

How George, who was my great, great, great, great, great grandfather, knew about the vacant smiddy, as the blacksmith's premises were called, is a mystery to me. He and his wife came from Carnbee in the East Neuk of Fife and local gossip does not travel that far. One possibility is that John Anstruther Thomson, who owned land both in Kilmany and at Charleton in the East Neuk of Fife, helped make the transfer possible.

But then it is also possible that Chalmers, who would have used blacksmiths to shoe his horses, would have had university contacts in the parish of Carnbee, which lies five miles south of St Andrew's. The reasons for George Wilson's arrival will remain a mystery, but the fact is he created the family base for the next one hundred and fifty years and the main line of work for the next seven generations of the family: blacksmiths.

Kilmany smiddy circa 1850 with
villagers posing for camera.

The smiddy, which was to be the workplace for the rest of his life, had wide sandstone walls and a pantile roof. As was the case in almost all village blacksmith premises, it sat immediately adjacent to the house in which he and his family lived. The house has nowadays been vastly extended and another storey added, but the original ground-floor walls and window openings are still basically the same as they were two hundred years ago. In the early years of the nineteenth century the blacksmith's house would have been like the majority of farm workers' and estate workers' homes, with no more than two rooms. Those houses used to be called 'but 'n' bens' in Scotland, one room being the but and the other referred to as the ben.

Small though the house was, it was the family home in which George and Betsy raised their two sons and a daughter, but then smaller houses and larger families were the norm in those days.

The smiddy was equally cramped, and with no door, it was open to the elements. Inside, it must have been pretty basic, with a fire, a pair of bellows and an anvil. Most of my ancestor's tools would have been brought with him or would, in time, have been made by himself. Village blacksmiths of two centuries ago were tool-makers for a large number of village-based trades and professions: spades, shovels and rakes were made for farm labourers, lasts were made for the village shoemaker and repairs were made on the looms used by the many linen-weavers in the rural parishes.

In the smiddy, there would be hooks on the rafters where partially made horseshoes would be hung. These were often made on quiet winter days and would come down off the hooks when the farmers and their workers brought their horses in to be shod in busier times with the coming of spring. Back then there were fourteen farms in Kilmany parish. The horses that required to be shod were mainly of the garron type, as the bigger, stronger Clydesdale had not been bred at that time.

While horseshoes can now be bought ready made, all the shoes in those days had to be hand made, as were the nails used to fix the metal shoes to the hoofs of the horses. The making or drawing of nails was always considered to be a job for the apprentice blacksmith. First the boy would form a head on the piece of metal and then draw out the shank, always remembering to put a slight angle on the nail. To this day, horseshoe nails have this slight angle to ensure that when they are hammered through the shoe into the hoof, the nail goes outward and not into the sensitive part of the foot. The length of those home-made nails would be judged just by eye, but woe betide any apprentice who wasted valuable metal by making them too long.

George Wilson might even had oxen to shoe, as they were used both to plough and as carters' animals. The feet of those cattle were shod with two half-cleat plates with nails on the outer edge, as the hoof wall is thin in comparison to that of a horse, and these plates too had to be hand made.

Basic farm machinery would also be made in the local smiddy, including the ploughs and harrows that were essential to the farming of that era. With all the machinery, each joint would have to be either forge welded or joined with bolts or rivets, and again, everything was hand made.

On the expenditure side, my five-times great grandfather would pay heavily for coal and iron, both essential to his work. There was no nearby coal mine or pit, meaning the coal for his forge would have to travel by horse and cart some eight or ten miles from a small shallow mine at Ceres, a village south of Cupar.

Another option was to buy coal brought in by ship to the village of Balmerino on the south side of the Tay. This English coal was reckoned to be higher quality but it was also more costly, especially during the winter time when it had to be brought by horse and cart over the hill to Kilmany. While blast furnaces in Central Scotland were producing tons and tons of pig iron in the early years of the nineteenth century to build railways and bridges, transport to Kilmany was limited. Any iron for the smiddy would have had to come in via the toll road that ran along the parish from Newport to Cupar. This road was not much used, with traffic preferring the less hilly road to Cupar or Dundee, a road which incidentally goes through Balmullo where my family and I now live. The metal for the blacksmith's use would have been brought in by carters who made a living bringing essentials to small communities such as Kilmany. A local parish history records foodstuffs such as bread being delivered by cart three days per week.

In country areas it was not unusual in those days for the blacksmith and other tradesmen such as shoemakers and weavers to receive some of the reward for their labours in non-cash agreements. Farm produce such as eggs, milk or potatoes were used in a barter system that operated on a small scale right up to within living memory. I myself recall my family receiving local farm produce.

In the early days of the nineteenth century, farming in Kilmany parish was mainly pastoral. Most of the land was open country with only a few fields around the farm buildings having hedges around them. Sheep and cattle were often grazed during the day on the outland, and tended by children who would bring the livestock home in the evening. Schooling was not compulsory in those days and child labour on small farms was taken for granted.

Bulky crops such as grain and potatoes were limited to what was needed for feeding the family. With no tarmacadam roads, haulage was both slow and expensive so such crops were only grown on the outskirts of towns. The exception to this was the growing of flax for making cloth and Kilmany had a number of weavers who would convert the flax into bales of cotton to be sold to merchants who came over from Dundee.

Within two years of George Wilson coming to Kilmany, farming fortunes rose with the introduction of the Corn Laws; they protected the home production of cereals against imported grain. Although there was no big acreage of grain grown in Kilmany, the economic ripple from this legislation brought more work for George Wilson as landowners were generally better off, more land went under the plough and more drainage schemes were carried out; the latter two activities had benefits for local blacksmiths through the selling of spades and shovels and the making of plough metal.

In Kilmany, there was a local sawmill that used the water from the Motray burn to power the saws, and there would also be work for the blacksmith from that business.

George Wilson's older son John, who was born in 1848, followed in his father's footsteps, although it might be more accurate to say he picked up his father's hammers and tongs. He must either have been a successful businessman or there was still a wave of prosperity in the countryside, as he took on two labourers to work in the smiddy. Not only did they work alongside him, but those two young apprentice blacksmiths also lived with John, his wife and their four children.

The most likely reason for the increased workload for the blacksmith would be the amount of machinery then being used in farming. Patrick Bell's reaper, or variations to it, and more efficient ploughs and cultivators were becoming more commonplace as farmers pushed for greater production. While these inventions removed some of the hard physical work of the harvest field, they also increased the work of the local blacksmith with repairs and spare parts.

The main railway line between Cupar and Dundee had been built in the 1870s and while the towns and villages close to the line were seeing the economic benefits from it, the rural parish of Kilmany was effectively bypassed by rail traffic until the early years of the twentieth century.

Roads had, however, improved, with Scotsman John McAdam pioneering a new system of upgrading the basic tracks between towns and villages. The new roads, which were made up of lots of small stones, were far superior to the rutted and potholed tracks. The newly macadamised roads were also much harder than the previous tracks. Consequently, horses' shoes wore down more quickly, requiring visits to the blacksmith to be reshod.

Ironically both the lack of a local railway and the increased road traffic were to the benefit of my ancestor as he and his men were called upon for the skilled work of making of iron rims for the wooden wheels of carts and carriages. To the present day, the frame of where these wheels were made lies outside the smiddy in Kilmany. This was usually a job for the winter months, as during the hot summer the wood contracted, and hard roads then caused the rim to expand.

John Wilson did not enjoy a long life, dying just before Christmas in 1888 aged sixty after suffering from asthma for many years. His youngest son George, then aged forty, took over the smiddy, his two elder siblings having died – John aged four died in 1859 of convulsions and Henry aged twenty-two in 1879, the death certificate attributing his demise to a 'softening of the brain'.

George's tenure of the smiddy coincided with a deep downturn in the fortunes of farming due to massive imports of food from countries all around the world. Grain came in from the newly discovered prairies of Northern America, and beef from South America in refrigerated boats, as did lamb from New Zealand and Australia. My great grandfather George Wilson, along with others in trades allied to farming, found to their cost that farmers tightened their financial belts by not spending any money. The old phrase of 'a pound spent off the farm is never seen again' was sadly proven to be true.

In 1905, such was the distressed state of the blacksmiths' business that they set up the Blacksmiths Association, which tried to establish a minimum price list and make everyone charge the same.

Kilmany smiddy 1905 with my grandparents and my
uncle standing on the ring for making cart wheels.

The turn of the century brought little economic relief, but the opening of the North British North Fife railway line in 1909 put Kilmany on the map. For the local blacksmith it also brought in coal and metal, both of which had previously been brought in expensively by carters. The new railway line was also a boon for farmers in the parish as they now potentially had a much larger market. Potatoes and other crops were transported by rail, and livestock could go to market in Dundee, which by this time had a large population. For dairy farmers, the morning train was able to take fresh milk right into towns.

The First World War brought dramatic changes to the country. Food imports were quickly reduced to a trickle as enemy boats sank ships bringing food into this country. Men joined up to fight, with an estimated one third of all eligible males going off to war. And the Army went round farms commandeering farm horses to help pull guns and supplies in the battlefields.

The effect on the blacksmith business was dramatic. Farmers were offered higher prices for their produce, and as soon as they had money in their pockets, they were prepared to pay more for horse shoeing and repairs.

Blacksmiths were also more than compensated for the reduction in working horses needing to be shod with the Army supplying the iron to make their horseshoes. The finished shoes would then be shipped off to the battlefields, to be fixed out there. My father used to recall how the nail holes in those shoes were inserted at an angle so that even the most amateur farrier could carry out the shoeing without injuring the horses.

However, when the Great War finished and hundreds of thousands of men returned from the Front to find there was no work, the country and the countryside slipped quickly into a deep economic depression.

Blacksmiths had to slash their prices for fear farmers would go to other farriers even if it meant a slightly longer journey for horse and man. It was in this economic recession that my grandfather retired in 1922. He must have been well regarded by the community as he was presented with a gold watch, and in handing it over, local landowner Colonel Anstruther-Gray described him as someone 'who did not have an enemy in the world'.

Sadly he did not enjoy a long retirement as he died only a couple of years later, but he did see the smiddy passed to my father, David Wilson, who was one of six siblings. Although it was never mentioned in the family, Dad had appeared in the local Sheriff Court as a young man, charged with shooting a rabbit, and had pleaded that he was just checking out the gun, which was an old fowling piece. He could have been fined a hundred pounds, which would have finished the business. The Sheriff took sympathy on him, though, as he was a man of the church and fined him one pound, with the option of spending five days in jail.

One of Dad's brothers went off to work as a grocer, but my uncle George also became a blacksmith. He worked at Ayton smiddy, which would, in due course, feature strongly in my own working life.

Kilmany smiddy with the house in which I was born
now grown into a two-storey building.

Explaining how the old-fashioned bellows used to work.

Apart from the economic woes of the 1920s and 1930s, my father's time as a blacksmith was marked by the change from real horsepower to mechanical horsepower. Steam engines had been around for a while but the introduction of tractors in the early years of the last century transformed farming. It also transformed the workload of a blacksmith: old horse-drawn machinery had to be converted to fit to the new tractors, which meant alterations to ploughs, seed barrows and even the horse-drawn binder.

There was another unexpected source of income, which came with the new roads. We now had council roadmen with their own stretch of road to maintain. They were called section men and took great pride in their work. Each individual's scythe had to be made up to the owner's precise settings. The blade had to be just right to enable them to shave the grass verges: if it was set too high the grass would be too long; too low, and they would dig into the ground. As all the roadmen were of a different height, all the scythes had to be individually adjusted and all the men in our vicinity came to the smiddy to fine tune their tools. When I think back to those pre-Health and Safety days, I am amazed to recall that the section men had bicycles and that they would carry their 'sharp as a razor' scythes wrapped round them as they cycled to and from work.

Tractors also brought another benefit to the blacksmith. Even in the early days of the last century, with ten- or twenty-horsepower engines these vehicles were so much more powerful than horses, and unlike horses, they did not stop when they hit a rock or misjudged a gate post. Often in the morning long before my father opened the smiddy to start work, an embarrassed farmer or farm worker would have left a heap of bent machinery outside the smiddy door for the blacksmith to straighten out.

We used to laugh at stories of horsemen who were let loose with a tractor for the first time. These men, so used to being in charge of their horses, had been heard to shout 'whoa' when they came to the end of a field. Sometimes to great hilarity in the neighbourhood, they landed in a burn or hit a wall.

As a young man I was also amused to listen to an elderly farmer trying to teach his old horseman to reverse a tractor. He would shout, 'Right hand down. Left hand down. Stop! You're going to hit the door.' This instruction would go on for quite a long time until it was mastered, or in some cases, never.

As a boy growing up in the post Second World War years, I soon found the smiddy was a great meeting place in the winter evenings, with the added bonus of a warm fire. The ploughmen would bring their plough socks, which is what the main wearing part of the plough is called, to be sharpened or 'laid'. This entailed forge welding a piece of metal onto the end of the sock when it wore down too far.

I remember one ploughman who had had his drill-plough sock repaired was not happy about how it was working, so he brought it back the next night. My father did not see anything wrong with it, so

Kilmany smiddy in the modern day.
Note the stone circle still in place.

he gave it a heat on the fire, made no alterations, and the man took it home saying it was now working perfectly. It was all in the mind.

The next advancement to the village smiddy turned out to be a real boon. Electricity came to Kilmany in 1952, the year I left school, and Dad bought an electric welder, drill and a buff for grinding down metal. This was for the next generation, as some of the older men, including Dad, never mastered the welder. They still preferred to work in the fire.

It seems amazing to recall that not long after electricity arrived, a local cattleman was cutting turnips with an electric cutter. He filled it up and then switched off the power, as he thought there would be enough electricity in the cable to finish the job.

If the first George Wilson could have travelled forward through time, he might have recognised the old forge but he would have been totally at a loss to see the other equipment around the smiddy.

Chapter 3

School and Sport

SOME rich children may have had their own playrooms in their big houses while children brought up on farms used to use the many sheds and buildings as their playground, but for me the smiddy, my father's workplace, was where I spent many happy hours. If my mother, Jeannie, wanted me out from under her feet as she cleaned our home, it was the easiest thing in the world to despatch me next door where my father was working.

It was here that I first practised my hammering technique. In one of my earliest memories, I remember sitting on the floor of the smiddy. With a handful of three-inch nails, I quickly learned I could hammer spare horseshoes onto the wooden railway sleepers that formed the floor. Whoever was working with Dad at that time then had to haul them out from the floor. I may not have realised it at the time, but that was my career established.

That was all to come, however. First of all there was schooling. Along with my sister Margaret and brother George, I went to the local school in Kilmany, which was all of a couple of hundred yards away from the family home. The school had only one classroom, and this one room had to cope with seven different classes. Pupils ranged from five years old up to eleven and Miss Morrison was the sole teacher for the school.

In the year above me there was a boy called Jim Clark, whose parents farmed Wester Kilmany farm. Jim later became a world champion Formula 1 driver. Tragically, he was killed racing in Germany, but even today, with twenty-five Grand Prix victories, he is regarded as one of the best racing drivers the world has ever known.

Nowadays his life is commemorated with a fine statue by local sculptor, David Annand. This statue, which is in Kilmany, was unveiled by Jackie Stewart, another world champion and legend in the motor-racing world. My schoolboy acquaintance with Jim Clark did not last long, as his family moved to a farm in the Borders in 1942.

The years went by and when I was eleven years old I, along six of the older pupils, was sent to neighbouring Rathillet school to finish my primary education. We travelled by bus the two miles from Kilmany to Rathillet, and initially this was a great adventure. The bus went round all the small villages, however, and, especially during the

With the late Jim Clark. Two world
champions and both born in Kilmany.

summer months, the return journey seemed to take an age, when all
we wanted to do was to throw off our school bags and go out to play.

We sometimes hitched a lift home in the grocery van that supplied
Kilmany and the outlying villages and farms. We had to step up into
the back of the van, which had shelves full of tins and lots of different
foods on either side, and then line up in the centre passage of the van,
the driver warning us not to 'touch the goods'.

In the long summer holidays from school, nothing much happened
in our sleepy little Kilmany. I spent days with my friends fishing with
a net and stick in the nearby Motray burn. The fish we caught were
kept alive and we sold them to Lady Kilmany who owned the local
estate. She then put them in her pond. I recall we used to receive
sixpence – in old money, which equates to two pence today – for a
big fish and a penny for the smaller ones.

That was altogether a better financial business than my first visit to
the burn with my mother and sister. Dad had lent me his fly fishing
rod. I think I was about eight years old at that time, and armed with
this fly rod, complete with flies, we walked down to the burn. First
cast I hooked my sister's finger. Tears flowed, I could see that was
the end of my day's fishing. My sister cried too, and we had to walk
home, me holding the rod and Margaret behind, still with the hook
attached until Dad managed to fish it out. No sixpence for that one.

It was a big shock to my system when in 1949 I started secondary
school at Bell Baxter High School in Cupar. After being in a school
with only around two dozen pupils, suddenly I was surrounded by

hundreds of other youngsters. They came from all the villages and small towns around Cupar.

Mostly, in similar fashion to me, they came in by bus. The seven-mile journey to and from my new school was often good fun and occasionally useful as we could do our homework before getting in to school. However, this was not easy as the buses back then were not as comfortable as they are now, especially the older ones with wooden seats. My already scratchy handwriting suffered as we bumped along the country roads.

At school, my favourite subject was physical education, or as everyone called it, PE. This was often carried out in the old gymnasium where there were all sorts of bits of exciting equipment such as rope ladders and wall bars, but I actually preferred the days when we went outside to play football.

Inside school, I liked technical subjects and maths. I remember on my first day in the metalwork room we had to file a piece of thin plate and the guy next to me made a screeching noise with his file. I cringed, which was all put on as I had heard it all before many a time in my father's smiddy. The teacher looked across the room and said, 'Wilson, there's still room in the gardening class.' I could so easily have ended up a gardener.

Bell Baxter school photograph. I am on the left in the second row.

Everyone of my vintage has a story to tell about getting the belt. The leather strap was the most common method of punishment in those days although it was almost always kept for administering to boys who misbehaved. Unlike others who can tell of getting 'six of the best' on numerous occasions, I think the only time I got the belt was in the woodwork class where, for some reason or other, someone sat on my knee. I opened up my legs and let him fall to the ground. The result was we both were belted.

By the time I was in the second year at Bell Baxter I was desperate for a bicycle, but this had to be worked for. The agreement I made with my dad was that I would work all the school holidays and my payment would be a bike. This agreement saw both of us heading into Cupar on the last Saturday of the holidays, where the first and as far as I was concerned the only stop was Leitch's bike shop.

Dad was keen for me to get a big strong Raleigh, but I had my eye on a B.S.A. racing bike. I got my choice and before any objections could be raised I was on the bike and heading off home to Kilmany. I had not gone far when I discovered the saddle was sharp. It was so painful that I had to get off about three times before I reached home. I was determined not to let on I had a sore backside even though I was asked several times why I was not keen to sit down. However, within two weeks I was able to ride my new racing bike for miles.

As I have mentioned, Kilmany was a quiet wee village so my weekends were often spent at nearby Luthrie, which may seem unusual as it was little bigger than my own hamlet. I used to slipstream behind the local buses as I soon found out that when I did, they would tow me along at forty miles per hour without any trouble. I remember once following the ten o'clock bus home one night when all of a sudden the bus brakes went on and it started to zigzag on the road. I almost ran in to the back of it. When we got to Kilmany, I asked the driver, whom I knew, what he was doing and he said, 'Sorry, I didn't know you were there, I was trying to get a rabbit for my dinner.'

That same bike lasted me from 1952 until 1962, when someone stole it, but that is a story I will come to later.

Another of my interests at high school was athletics. I took up running and soon found out my best distances were the half mile and the mile. I used to train on the local railway line where, by running on every third sleeper, I quickly developed an even stride. My usual training run would see me run from the house down to the bridge at the Kilmany school, on to the railway line and then along to Cruivie bridge, which carried a small road over the railway. Then it was back onto the road and home. This was about one and a half miles altogether, which I did about three times a week.

My first success on this training regime came when I won the Bell Baxter school mile. This race was open to all the school, with the fifth and sixth years starting off from scratch. I was in the third year and got about fifty yards of a start while the first and second years were given a bigger handicap. I still recall the thrill I got when passing the older boys and going on to win the race.

My next race was a two-mile boys' marathon at Ceres Games, where I came second. This was the first time I received any financial reward and even although it was only two pounds it was quite an incentive as I then won a mile race at the Cupar Highland Games and pocketed three pounds.

Over the following years, I ran all over the country, winning my fair share of races entered. All the races were run on a handicap basis and I had to watch out and just win, as it seemed to me the handicapper was always looking for reasons to give all the other competitors a bigger start.

Not long after I started to work for Dad in the smiddy, I found out that the Arbroath Highland Games were to be held on a Monday. Although this was in the working week, I was desperate to go, but Dad was not keen. After a great deal of moaning on my part, he relented and off I went.

At that time my wages were two pounds per week, but after a successful day on the track I came home with fifteen pounds from the Games. It was made up with ten pounds for winning the half mile and

Captain of Bell Baxter under-fifteen football team.

five for coming second in the mile. I reckoned it was a good day's work.

If running was my summer sport, the winter months would see me on a football field. I was captain of the school under-fifteen team when we went on to win the Fife Schools Cup. Not content with playing on Saturday mornings for the school, I then went and played for Gauldry amateur team in the afternoons. Today I do not know how I managed that hectic schedule as it often included cycling there and back. I can only conclude that it was great to be young and fit.

One reason for cycling along to Luthrie whenever I could was that basically there were not many boys of my age in Kilmany with whom I could play.

My best pal, Dave Brown, actually came from Larbert. His grandmother was the postmistress in Kilmany and he came to stay with her every weekend as well as during all the school holidays.

We had been talking about various ploys when, for some unremembered reason, we decided that we would keep racing pigeons. I converted one of my dad's sheds at the back of the house and scrounged some pigeons from friends. Dave did the same. He always seemed to have extra money, so we bought a new Toulet pigeon clock. This was a big investment. As I remember, it cost twenty-two pounds plus the carriage from England.

Our next step on our flight to what we hoped would be to the top of the pigeon-racing world came in 1952 when we joined Leuchars Pigeon Club. We flew our birds under the name of Wilson and Brown. The new firm bred about thirty young birds each year, fitting them with identification rings as soon as they reached about seven days old. We then started training these birds when they were around four and a half months old.

The training was a case of putting the young birds in wicker baskets and then these containers were put into the boot of a car, which was driven by whoever was available at the time. On arrival at the planned destination, the birds were released. Initially the release point would only be a short distance away, but then gradually the range increased as the young birds gained experience.

After they could fly home from a radius of about twenty miles, the birds were transported by train. At that time trains still stopped at Kilmany. I recall there was a special label put on the pigeon basket, asking the station master to liberate the birds from the chosen station and to return the basket. The train would go along the local line for a couple of miles from Kilmany to St Fort, at which point the pigeons in their baskets would be transferred to the mainline train, to go to the station we had requested, probably Kirkcaldy or even Haymarket in Edinburgh.

On a race night, we would take the birds to the Leuchars club, which had about twelve members at that time. Each pigeon had a rubber ring, containing a race number, fitted over its leg. This race number would be registered opposite the unique identifier of that pigeon.

Then all the birds, maybe as many as two or three hundred, would be put into big baskets each holding approximately thirty. These baskets were loaded onto the guard's van on the train going to the release point. The train would then pick up all the rest of the baskets from the pigeon clubs throughout Fife. A representative from the Fife Federation of Pigeons accompanied the birds on the train, and was responsible for their welfare.

Next day, all the baskets were laid out on the platform, the strings tying the baskets were cut and all the birds were liberated together. Trains have not been used in recent times for transporting pigeons, as the various federations now use large, specially adapted lorry transporters that carry hundreds of birds.

After the birds were released, the secretary from the Federation used to telephone all the club secretaries, notifying them of the liberation

Admiring one of my pigeons. It had just won a race.

With Mairi after a successful pigeon-racing season.

time and the wind direction. From that information, we fanciers, as racing-pigeon keepers are called, knew approximately when to start watching for our birds coming home.

When a bird comes back, it must enter the loft for the fancier to remove the rubber ring, which is then put into a thimble and inserted into the pigeon clock. This provides the accurate time of the bird's arrival.

Just as happens today, before the race started, the distance from the release point would have been measured to each individual fancier's loft. The result is then calculated by working out distance travelled over time taken. The result can be very close as the time the pigeon is on the wing is taken down to the nearest second and the distance is calculated to sixtieths of a yard. The result appears as yards per minute, and stating the obvious, the pigeon flying the most yards per minute wins the race.

I have kept pigeons most of my life with the exception of one break, and that was when I proposed to my future wife. I was not well off, and since money was in short supply, I decided to sell all my pigeons to buy an engagement ring. This, in my mind, was true love.

According to family folklore, the day after our wedding I bought them back, but this is not quite true. I had given some birds free to a fancier, with the promise that if I ever wanted to start again, I would get my own strain of pigeon back.

Unfortunately for him, due to unforeseen circumstances, he had to give up the sport and I ended up with the pigeons being returned sooner than expected. I have had them ever since.

Over the years, I have had quite a lot of success both at club and national levels, having had birds fly non-stop for over fifteen and a half hours from France. Sometimes they have been competing against four or five thousand other birds. It is not easy to win when some of the fanciers are flying almost a hundred miles less than the fanciers in this part of Scotland, as birds tend to get tired on the 'last lap'.

However, I remain hopeful that one day one of my birds will win the Gold Cup, which is the premier race, starting in France, some 575 miles from Balmullo. Apart from the prestige of winning, the prize money is over two thousand pounds.

Keeping pigeons did, however, lead to one of my more unusual jobs. As we prepared our birds for one particular race, an elderly fancier saw me trimming one of my fingernails, which had become ragged. I was using the only trimmers to hand, which were a pair of eighteen-inch hoof cutters that I would usually use for trimming horses' feet.

He asked could I come to his house and cut his toenails, as he could not get his slippers on. I said, 'Go home and wash your feet and I will come along later.' It must have been quite funny to see me holding his leg like a horse's foot, but having made a good job, I was asked to do this every six weeks.

Over the years my pigeons have been a welcome form of relaxation from a busy working life, and are a hobby I enjoy to this day, although sadly in recent years I have had more bird losses than was the case when I started out fifty years ago. Whether this is due to all the mobile telecommunication signals or increased numbers of birds of prey, it is difficult to say. All I know is that it is a fact.

Chapter 4

Starting Work

FOR many youngsters starting a first job is a major step. It is the hurdle you cross when you move from being a child into an adult. It is also the first entry into earning your own keep as opposed to just receiving pocket money.

Well, that may be the view of the majority, but as far as I was concerned the transition from child to adult was hardly earth shattering. Basically, I left school on Friday for the Easter holidays and started work the following Monday morning. Nothing out of the ordinary, as throughout my schooling I was in and out of my father's smiddy on a daily basis, and especially at the weekends where it became part of my play area.

I cannot recall there being any discussion as to what I was going to do with my life. It just seemed to be expected that I would become the sixth-generation Wilson to be a blacksmith, and that suited me.

My sister, Margaret, was the oldest of my siblings, and morning and night she would cycle the three miles or so to and from the nearest train station where the train took her to work in Dundee. George, the only other contender to follow in his father's footsteps as a blacksmith, went off to train as a civil engineer, a profession that saw him start work with the local authority in Cupar. Various promotions and moves later he retired as chief engineer for Lothian Region.

When I entered the smiddy, there was still a real novelty in switching on the electric light, this new form of power only having been installed in Kilmany about three months before I started.

Having spent my schooldays watching my father working in winter time with only the light from the fire in the forge alongside a couple of old 'hurricane' lamps that hung from the rafters, the immediate burst of light from electricity was remarkable.

But more impressive in my eyes was the fact that electricity also powered an electric welder and a buff used in grinding metal. It was my job to weld, and in this I was aided by tutors from Scottish Rural Industry. These men visited the smiddy to teach electric and gas welding and wrought iron-work to young apprentice blacksmiths.

Much of the horse machinery used on farms had already been converted to be pulled by tractors. This work involved the old horse shafts being taken off carts, and drawbars suitable for tractors being

31

The Wilson family. From the left: sister Margaret,
brother George, Dad, myself and Mum.

fitted. There was a great deal of this work to be done as farms moved
to mechanical horsepower.

It suited me that Dad remained as an old-style blacksmith, more
comfortable working with the forge and the fire. He could weld
things that I would not attempt even now, having done fire welding
all his life.

A large part of my first months in the smiddy was spent repairing
harrows, which in the 1950s were still a major cultivating tool on farms.
Two, three and occasionally four leaves made up a set of harrows,
with every leaf holding twenty tines to knock the soil into a condition
suitable for sowing. The trouble was that all the scraping through the
soil wore the tines down, and then it was a case of dropping the worn
harrows off at the blacksmiths for repair or renewal.

To do this required all the tines to be taken out of the frame and
then sharpened or laid. This process entailed fire welding a new piece
of five-eighth square iron onto the existing tine. The next step was to
resharpen the tine before it was put back into the frame.

I may have silently cursed this early labour as boring and repetitive
as well as being hard work but it certainly taught me how to fire weld,
and that training has stood me in good stead throughout my life.

I was also learning how to shoe horses, despite there being no official or college training at that time. In those early post-war years, there were still a few horses being worked in the area and some of the farmers and landowners had hunting horses or ponies.

My first encounter with horses did not go well. I was asked to go out and shoe a horse on a nearby farm, but no one had told me I had to catch it first. It was running freely in quite a big field. Several times I chased it around the field trying to corner it but these efforts were unsuccessful. I did learn that if in future someone wanted their horse shod, they either had to meet me at the field with the horse already haltered or in the stable or shed with a nice clean floor. This was not always possible, but there is nothing worse than having to shoe a horse in the winter time in mud, rain or even sometimes snow. It is little wonder that farriers have a reputation of being bad tempered.

Sadly I was not long into the job before my dad's health began to fail and he spent a lot of time in bed. I could still ask his advice, but mostly I had to work a problem out myself. By this time I was driving and had almost enough knowledge to go out to deal with a lame horse that was unable to walk to the smiddy. Or at least I thought I had.

Dad's illness took a turn for the worse and he went into hospital. As well as having a heart condition, he also contracted a salmonella infection and suffered a massive heart attack. He died on 1 January 1955, little more than two years after I had joined him in the smiddy.

My mother and I decided to try and carry on with the business. This was hard for me as I was only seventeen years old and without the knowledge needed to keep the business going on my own. Thankfully, I had help from various people, including my uncles, who were all

Leaving for work in my overalls with
brother George in shirt and tie.

Working at home with my father.

in the trade and worked in neighbouring smiddies. I kept working away, learning all the time about horses and also, and possibly more importantly, about people.

This may all be beginning to sound like a tale of woe, so I should say that there were quite a few amusing times with some of the characters who came into the smiddy.

One of these saw a farmer, who was built like a weightlifter, lift up and carry the anvil outside, where he dumped it before jumping in his car and driving away. The anvil weighed about two hundredweight, or a hundred kilos, and I had to work outside on it until someone came and helped me lift it back inside and onto its stand.

Although working horses had virtually disappeared by the second half of the 1950s, Lord Kilmany, one of the local landowners, had his racing stable in operation at this time and I now had racehorses to shoe. Despite my limited knowledge, I got by.

Meanwhile in non-working hours I kept on with my athletic training at nights in order to be really fit for the Highland Games. I also had my pigeons to look after, so I did not have a lot of spare time.

At that point another diversion came into my life and although I did not know it at the time, it was to change and enrich my existence.

The night before Ceres Highland Games in 1955, the organisers held a dance in the local hall. I had borrowed the family car, which needed petrol that I could get in the local town. The dilemma was that although the smiddy had a petrol account and I did not have to pay for the fuel, I had no money with me.

By chance, I met two girls whom I knew. They were waiting for a bus to go to the dance. I stopped to chat to them and came to an agreement that I would drive them to the dance if they paid for me to get in.

After a few dances, I asked this beautiful dark-haired girl for a dance. Later on, she asked me up for ladies' choice and low and behold, Mairi and I are still together after fifty-nine years.

Meanwhile things got difficult in the smiddy and Mum and I finally decided that I needed more experience. At the same time, Jock McKenzie, who had served his apprenticeship with Dad, was in need of someone to work with him, and so everyone thought the best idea would be for me to finish my apprenticeship with him along the road at Ayton.

A sale of all the tools and bits and pieces of equipment in the Kilmany smiddy was organised. Such events are called roups and they generally attract large crowds. Some of those who turn up are merely curious visitors; some see a roup as a social occasion, but the people you really want to come along are those who will bid for the tools and machinery.

Preparing for the sale was quite an experience. I knew all the gear that was in everyday use but when I started to dig back into the recesses of the smiddy, I came across various items that my ancestors must have used in some bygone era.

Unless it was for shooting a rabbit for the pot, I have no idea why my father or grandfather still owned an old muzzle-loading gun. Perhaps it had been hidden away after his appearance in court in the 1920s for shooting a rabbit. Along the same shelf as the gun were a brass powder cask and a couple of muzzle loaders. Then, to complete the armoury, there were moulds for making lead shot.

We had not heard of antiques in those days and the guns and their loaders just went into the sale. If I remember correctly, the auctioneer knocked them down for little more than pennies.

The vagaries of selling or buying at an auction were never more clearly illustrated to me when it came to selling the anvils. There were four in the smiddy and as is the custom, the best one was to be sold first, the theory being it will set a high trade for the rest.

The first, which I had used right up to the sale, came under the hammer, but the bidding was slow and it was knocked down for a pound. The auctioneer moved on to sell the second-best anvil and he got the price up to two pounds before dropping the hammer. The third went for the same price but when the last and poorest one came up for sale, the bidding rose to four pounds.

One of the customs at a roup or a waygoing is that the neighbours like to 'get their name' on the roup roll, or sales sheet. Normally this is some small tool such as a spade or a shovel or brush. I can only think the buyer of the last anvil was either generous in his support, or through being overly cautious he had missed out on the earlier ones.

For me the sale day just passed in a whirl, with neighbours, friends and relations all around, helping, buying or just chatting; the little smiddy and the road outside it had never been as busy.

But with the last item sold, the busy-ness soon shifted to quietness. The new owners took their purchases home, each one leaving the little smiddy just that little bit emptier.

By nightfall on that November day, the building that had been a work place for my family for the best part of a century and a half was quiet and still and empty of life.

I was only eighteen years old and I did not fully realise it was the ending of an era. Well, it was not quite the ending, as Lord Kilmany, the local landowner and keen huntsman, had bought the best anvil so that his horses could be shoed locally. In the coming years, I occasionally went to Kilmany with my employer, Jock McKenzie, to carry out the work, and I used the old anvil originally owned by my family.

I began work at Ayton smiddy on the following Monday morning. This was a shock to the system, as I had to cycle seven miles each way from Kilmany to Ayton. The road was almost straight, but by some quirk of the weather, the wind always seemed to be in my face.

After a few weeks of work at Ayton, I had managed to save some money. I then invested it in a motorbike, which made travel a lot less stressful. I always seemed to be in a last-minute rush to work, and my boss, Jock, always reckoned that if the bike did not start first kick of the starter, then I would be late. But I don't think that was exactly true.

When I arrived at Ayton that first day, there were forty sets of harrows up against the railway fence, all to be repaired. It was as if they had been saved up, waiting for me to arrive.

As I had learned with my father, the harrow work was monotonous and time consuming. It was also extremely hard graft, especially if new tines were required, as they needed a screw head to fit them to the harrow. This introduced me to a new skill, as the thread was screwed on with a hand-screwing machine, which was very hard work.

I think it took about three months to get through the heap of harrows but again it taught me not just to work hard but also to be efficient. I learned to make every blow with the hammer count and I also found the truth in the old saying of striking while the iron was hot.

As I grew older and gained more experience, I spent more time repairing combines and balers, servicing them before harvest began and also carrying out emergency repairs when the heat of harvest was on when it was essential to keep them working until everything was cut and baled.

I always had lunch with Jock and his wife Irene. To this day, she reminds me about a goose she was once given, which had been shot by a local farmer. I had been delegated to pluck the bird, and started off with great gusto pulling out the feathers.

After appearing to get nowhere, I took the oxygen and acetylene burner and burned all the feathers off. Sadly this spark of invention on my part did not deal with the quills, which were left in the carcass, and the bird was burned black. Not at all edible, so not many plus marks that day.

After Mairi and I had been going out for two years, I reckoned that it was now time to ask her dad's permission to marry his daughter. Thankfully I received a positive response, as I would not have argued with him – a man of six foot three.

We were engaged in June 1957 but just in case there is a feeling that this has turned into a romantic novel, the engagement came just before Dundee Highland Show, at which I would be competing in the apprentice shoemaking class.

To celebrate our engagement, we thought we would have a week's holiday in Skye where Mairi's family has its roots. In order to get there, we bought a car. The old Ford had come out of the factory in 1932, so it had a few miles on the clock before it came into our life.

To smarten the old banger up a bit, Mairi's mum made covers for the interior, and I painted the outside as well as checking the engine. Mairi and I each put five pounds in the kitty to cover the total cost of ten pounds for the vehicle.

The next weekend we set off for Skye. Mairi's mum was going up too, but she wisely went by train. Our departure was delayed because we had only travelled about two hundred yards before one of the doors burst open. It was one of those doors that opened out backwards and so I tied a rope from one handle around the steering column and across to the other door to hold it closed.

We then set sail on our two hundred-and-fifty-mile journey, thankful that there was no such thing as MOT testing in those days.

We did get to Skye, but unfortunately when we were there the dynamo packed up and we ended up buying a new one for eleven pounds. It actually cost us more than the car.

That was not all our mechanical problems, as at another point in our travels the car battery conked out and Mairi had to push the car in the pouring rain. Her hands were cold and she lost her brand-new engagement ring. We were fortunate that a tour bus had stopped at the petrol station where we were looking, and when the passengers heard about it, they all came out and helped in the search. Thankfully the ring was found by the bus driver. I quietly thought I had had a narrow escape.

Soon it was time to head home and after getting the car battery charged up, we headed back to Fife. It went like a dream until we got to some fifteen miles from Perth when the engine blew up. As I lifted the bonnet, it did not require a great deal of engineering knowledge to conclude that the connecting rod of the piston had gone right through the engine block. We abandoned our car and arrived back in Cupar on the bus. Not, you might say, quite the perfect end to a lovely week's holiday.

Meanwhile work continued as usual at the smiddy. We were now making turnip-cutting carts for chopping up turnips for sheep, and orders for this mechanical invention were being taken from well beyond the immediate neighbourhood. At the same time, Jock decided to build a new workshop, so we also had all the steelwork to make for that.

In 1958, Mairi and I decided to get married. As everyone who has taken the step into married life can confirm, it can be quite a shock to cast aside bachelor ways, but I confess being married has been the best thing to have happened to me.

We arranged to rent a cottage on a farm just along the road from the smiddy. This was going to suit us perfectly, but at the last minute, there was a change of plan.

The estate that owned the farm where the cottage was situated had decided to sell the whole property, along with Jock's smiddy and the smiddy house, which were also in its ownership. Fortunately, Jock managed to buy the house that we were going to rent, as well as his own property and the smiddy. Unfortunately this transaction took over a month to be finalised, so we spent the first months of our married life in Cupar with my in-laws.

For our honeymoon we booked a hotel in Inverness, but after about three days there we found it was so awful that we left. Our next stop was Mairi's family home in Skye, where we spent the rest of our holiday.

For travel we had hired a Standard Vanguard and found it would pass everything except a petrol pump. Etched on my memory is the fact that we used thirty-nine gallons of petrol in that one week. At that time, petrol may only have cost five shillings, or twenty-five pence per gallon, but it was a serious item of expenditure for a trainee blacksmith.

The following Monday, I went back to work as a married man. The old car had gone and I now had a van. The house at Balmeadie was soon ready for us to move into, so the van came in very handy for moving our few bits and pieces.

To begin with our new home had no electricity, but it was quite a novelty for us to use paraffin lamps, candles and a lovely coal fire. With the flush of young love we were very comfortable and cosy.

All of our cooking was done on a gas cooker and there was a big boiler in the corner of the kitchen that supplied hot water for washing. Beside the boiler was an old-fashioned scrubbing board.

Our first daughter was born in 1959 in St Andrews, where Mairi had to spend six weeks. Margaret MacKinnon Wilson eventually arrived weighing in at nine pounds.

We settled well into family life and had a routine of working, washing nappies, as there were no such things as disposable nappies in those days, and all the other chores that come with having children.

The smiddy was very busy and I had to work a lot of overtime. It was good financially to get the extra overtime cash but it meant Mairi and the baby were on their own a lot, so we decided to get a dog. On one of the neighbouring farms, there was a shepherd who used to go to sheepdog trials and he had a pup that was about ten months old. It was also, allegedly, very well bred.

Unfortunately, it was not a family dog and was very nervous indoors. If the clock chimed, the dog dived under the table. Soon the dog had Mairi as nervous as itself.

Thankfully, not long after, the shepherd lost one of his dogs and asked if he could have his dog back, which suited us just fine. We then bought a little West Highland terrier, which turned out be a perfect companion, and we had Minky for many years until she died aged fourteen.

In another move, the man to whom I gave my pigeons contacted me to say he was moving out of the area and wanted to give me my pigeons back. This was much sooner than anticipated. However, I quickly converted an old outside toilet into a pigeon loft until I had time to build a proper home for them. Keeping the birds in the old toilet block meant I could claim I owned the only pigeon loft with running water.

In 1960, our second daughter, Ann, made her appearance at Craigtoun Hospital, but Mairi was only in hospital for one week this time.

Life settled into a routine that could be easily described as busy at home and busy at work. Our annual holidays were always spent in Skye, where I could do a bit of fishing for relaxation as well as enjoy valuable family time.

Another two years later, our family was again increasing. This time Mairi was going to have the baby at home, with the doctor and district nurse in attendance. I was supposed to take a week off, but kept working until the baby arrived.

Donna weighed in at ten pounds and one ounce. The doctor stopped in at the smiddy to tell me about the newest addition to the family and then he went on his way back to Cupar. I jumped on my bike and pedalled home as fast as I could, throwing the bike against the hedge as I dashed in to see Mairi and our new daughter.

I spent the week helping in the house, washing nappies, cooking and generally doing domestic chores. By this time we had electricity and a washing machine, so things were much easier.

After a week of this, I was ready to go back to work for a rest. I went out ready to jump on my bike but it was gone. Someone had stolen it: stolen my trusty old bike that I had owned for fifteen years a bike that had seen me first as a schoolboy and lastly as a father of three fine daughters.

Having a wife and family, I started to think of my career prospects, so I applied for a mechanic's position down in England, servicing combines and balers. I was asked down for an interview, which, even if I say it myself, went well.

However, later after lots of discussions at home, we decided that we really wanted to stay in Scotland, so I withdrew my application. We then started to look for a place of our own where I could start a business. I had enjoyed my time at Ayton and Jock and I remained friends, competing together in shoeing competitions for many years after.

Mairi, three daughters, a West Highland dog, some pigeons and I had come to the end of one part of my life, but it also was the start of another.

Chapter 5

Starting Off in the Competitive World

WHILE I had watched my father making and fitting horseshoes from my earliest days, I had also made a few of my own, both under his supervision and on my own after his illness and death.

Despite that background, I would not have called myself anything more than proficient at the job. After all, the number of working horses in the mid 1950s was only a fraction of what it had been right up to the Second World War.

Only after I started to work with Jock McKenzie at Ayton did I really begin to hone the skills needed to be a good competition blacksmith. It was back in the depths of winter in 1955 that we hatched a plan that would see me compete at the Highland Show the following summer. Jock was an old hand and had already competed at this, the top agricultural event in Scotland.

The Highland Show is run by the Royal Highland and Agricultural Society, which was set up two hundred years ago to improve education and advance agriculture. Back in the 1950s it was still a travelling show moving around the various regions of Scotland; a costly exercise that only came to an end with the purchase of a permanent base at Ingliston just outside Edinburgh in 1960. However, in 1956 the venue was to be Inverness.

As part of our preparation for the competition, from February onwards Jock and I would make a pair of shoes each once a week. This work was done at night as time during the day was too precious.

In order to get into the rhythm of working together, a great deal of preparation had to be undertaken. The training also disciplined me into working within the tight time limits that were an important part of the competition.

As spring wore on, I started to pick up the benefits of our working together. While we had talked a lot in our early training sessions, we soon knew each other's moves without having to speak. Other, that is, than the times when one of us got it wrong, and then there was plenty to say.

As the time approached, the excitement grew. Quite apart from feeling ready to compete, there was also the fact that this was a whole new world opening up for me. What would the other competitors be like? What would I feel and how would I react with lots of people watching us making the shoes? Would I have time to sleep with those and a dozen other unanswered questions rattling around my head?

Instead of worrying about the competition and all the novelties around it, perhaps I should have been concentrating on how I would actually get there. With no suitable transport myself, I borrowed my brother's motorbike. He was in the Army at the time and it is quite possible I never got round to asking his permission to take it.

I picked up Jock at Ayton smiddy, and complete with all the tools we needed we set off on the bike. Some ten miles up the road, just south of Perth, we had arranged to meet Bob Millar, another blacksmith, who worked out of Dunshalt smiddy. Because the bike was seriously overloaded, the plan had been for Jock and the tools to be transferred into Bob's car.

I had never been to Inverness before so it was agreed I should follow the car. Unfortunately the bike kept breaking down. Most times, this misfortune was quickly picked up by the occupants of the car, who turned round and helped get me back on the road again, but on one occasion they had driven on several miles before realising they were not being tailed by a biker. Bob did not hide his disgust at the intermittent progress and I think at one point he threatened to leave me. But soon we crested the last hill and saw the Moray Firth in front with Inverness snuggled in as the water narrowed into the Beauly Firth.

Our journey may have been over but our next problem was that we had not thought of booking any accommodation. Undaunted, we decided to sleep in the big tent erected for the competition, along with a number of other blacksmiths. A few bales of straw were borrowed from the neighbouring cattle stalls, then opened up and scattered on the ground. Our accommodation was sorted, as the straw provided our bed for the night.

With all the excitement of the travel now behind me, I was soon asleep in the makeshift bed. Little did I or any of my sleeping companions know that the tent had been erected right next to the poultry section. I needed no alarm clock as, at first light, all the cockerels started to crow. Their noise, plus the excitement of this being my first show, kept me from any further sleep, so my first experience of a Highland Show came before anyone else was up.

By half past six, one of the smiddy fires had been lit and within minutes bacon and eggs were sizzling in the pan. It is often said that the smell of bacon frying is one of the most mouthwatering experiences. That might be the case, but the aroma of bacon did not rouse one competitor. Jimmy Walker from Strathkinness was nowhere to be seen as the rest of the blacksmiths tucked in to breakfast. Eventually he was uncovered after we found him in a corner of the tent, still covered with straw.

After our hearty breakfast, I had to get ready for the junior competition. With the decline of the workhorse on farms, blacksmiths were not taking on apprentices, the net result being that there were only two competitors in my class: myself and another lad who came from outside Keith and who had competed the previous year, so he was an experienced competitor in my eyes.

About fifteen minutes before the competition was due to start, we drew lots for the fires. Jock built up the fire with the special coal used in smiddy fires. It is different from household coal as it is small, being a maximum of three quarters of an inch in diameter, and is washed to remove any dust as this can affect the metal.

The stewards, who were also the timekeepers, handed over my two iron bars for making the front and rear shoes along with the square of metal that I had to forge weld on to the toe of the hind shoe. I marked the iron in the middle, as that would be where the toe of the shoe would be. I noticed my hands were shaking badly

Competing in the junior class in Inverness at my first Highland Show in 1956, with Jock McKenzie keeping a watchful eye.

with nerves. However, as soon as the bell sounded for the start, my nerves vanished, with Jock starting to heat the bars for me and telling me firmly to 'Just remember and do it as we practised.'

With that advice ringing in my ears, I found it easy to get into the rhythm needed and soon the bars of metal were being hammered into shape.

Meanwhile I could hear the timekeeper giving a countdown as we were working. His voice rang out with military precision: 'Fifteen minutes to go,' 'Ten minutes to go,' and then, seemingly only seconds later, 'Five minutes.'

By this time panic was setting in and I found myself thinking, 'will I get finished on time?' Later someone asked me if I heard or saw all the people watching the competition. I can honestly say I never saw a soul, especially in the few remaining minutes as I strove to finish the shoes. As the countdown came to the last seconds with sweat flying from my brow, I recall giving the shoes one last blow from the hammer to make sure they were level. As the final bell sounded, I did as had been drummed into me and dropped the tools I had in my hand. Just as all competitors do, I looked at the shoes I had just finished and thought to myself, 'mine are not too bad,' but then it would be up to the judges to decide that, and I would have to wait on their verdict.

Because I was in the first round in the morning, I had the rest of the day to myself, so I had a good look around the show. My first port of call was the poultry section, but I could not identify any of the cockerels that had woken me at the crack of dawn. Later I went back to the blacksmiths' tent and spent the rest of the day watching the senior men making their shoes. Jock had Bob heating and striking for him – I could have done it but don't think he trusted me then, as I was only a boy. In later years, that changed and he and I competed successfully at many, many events.

Soon it was time for the judges to give their verdict on the day's competition and their decision placed me in second place; that sounds much better than coming last.

As that was the only class in which I had been entered, it was time for me to go home, leaving the seniors with another couple of days of competition. All went well on the first half of the trip back south, but by the time I got down to Bruar, my brother's old motorbike decided it had gone far enough and it just stopped.

Luckily, someone I knew who lived close to my home in Fife came upon the broken-down bike and the stranded young blacksmith and they stopped to offer help. We soon had a rope tied to the tow bar and the bike's handlebars and I sat on the bike as he towed me to the nearest house. There I abandoned the bike and went home in the relative comfort of his car.

I knew my brother would be less than happy to be told his bike had broken down and been abandoned on some farm in Perthshire, so the next day I borrowed a local farmer's Land Rover to bring the wounded bike back. At that time of my life, Mairi was still my girlfriend, and possibly putting her love for me to the test, I asked if she would come with me to retrieve the bike. Happily, the experience of dealing with broken-down motorbikes did not put the young lady off our romance, as she has now been my wife for more than half a century.

So far I have not mentioned the financial implications of my first competition at the Highland Show. They can easily be summarised as my prize money being totally spent on the twelve gallons of petrol I needed to buy for the borrowed Land Rover.

Far from being discouraged by coming second I resolved that next year, I would show the rest of the competitors if not a clean pair of heels at least a top-class pair of horse shoes.

If there is such a thing as a home match, 1957 saw the Highland

Competing at the 1957 Highland Show with Jock McKenzie.

Show pitch up in Riverside Drive, Dundee, less than ten miles away from Kilmany as the crow flies but more if you were a human being having to use either the train or the ferry to get over the river Tay.

With my ambition to do better and with the experience of my first Highland competition behind me, I started practising with Jock early in the spring.

When the show opened in mid-June, we took the train from Kilmany station to Dundee West station, which is now closed but was within walking distance of the show.

I soon found out there was extra competition in 1957 as the number of apprentices competing had risen to three. However, the extra practice must have helped as I finished up in first position.

Mairi and I were engaged by that time, and for the show week she was a receptionist in the Fisons Tent where the fertilizer company dished out hospitality to its farmer and merchant customers. More than half a century on from that time, I think it is safe to confess that I used to take some of the other horseshoeing competitors round to the Fisons hospitality tent for a free coffee and sausage roll.

That was the last year I was able to compete in the apprentice class as it was restricted to those under twenty-one years old.

Next year I would be in with the big boys.

Chapter 6

Now with the Big Boys

THE Royal Mile in Edinburgh has that regal name because the famous Edinburgh Castle stands at one end and Holyrood Palace, the official Royal residence in Scotland, at the other. Nowadays, the Scottish Parliament also lies adjacent to it on the former site of Queensberry House.

I mention this purely because, in 1822, the first ever Highland Show was held in the grounds of Queensberry House, and according to the newspaper reports of the event, somewhere between sixty and seventy-five cattle were exhibited along with eight new Leicester sheep and 'two beautiful pigs'.

Back in Kilmany, my six-times great grandparent would have been working in his forge, dealing with the everyday business of a village blacksmith. It was the turn of the twentieth century before blacksmiths competed at the Highland Show, and it was in 1960 that the Highland show came back to Edinburgh for good with a permanent site at Ingliston, close to the city's airport.

The arrival of the show at its permanent base did not reduce the fellowship and camaraderie that we competitors had enjoyed at the various touring shows. If anything, the nonsense and fooling about increased as we settled in to the new premises.

That first year on the permanent site saw all the blacksmiths gathered in the evening at the forge where we would be competing. We went for a walk round the show via the Herdsman's bar, which has traditionally been the big meeting point for exhibitors and competitors at the show.

About midnight, we returned to the shoeing stand and someone lit one of the forge fires. For a joke, a piece of iron about five feet long was put in to heat. Then things began to get serious.

A suggestion was made that we should make a massive horseshoe from the iron bar. Tools were brought out and we started, with everyone doing their part. The younger ones, including myself, did the sledge-hammer work and the senior men made the shoe. When one person tired, the next in line took over. The end result of this combined 'after midnight' session of tomfoolery was a horseshoe perfect in every detail for some massive, mythical equine.

By the time we were finishing it was nearly two o'clock in the morning and because the shoeing stand was in the centre of the showground, word had gone around and the old canvas tent was full of spectators, enthralled by this impromptu display. Police inspectors and firemasters were in the crowd, but no one complained as no harm was being done and all the competitors were delighted when they received a big round of applause for their efforts when they finished.

After this extra late-night session, where no overtime was asked or paid for, it was a case of heading straight to bed, wherever we were sleeping, in order to get some rest for the competitions the next day. We had not been allowed to erect a large tent for sleeping in as had been our custom during the travelling Highland Show era, so we all had to make our own arrangements. Initially, I and many of the other competitors slept in our vans, but later most of us bought or rented caravans. In the early years at Ingliston, two of the hardier individuals used to sleep on a mattress between the fires but such informal sleeping arrangements are now frowned on and have become a thing of the past.

What happened to the huge shoe? It was presented to one of the judges, Willie Stephen from Turriff, who in turn gave it to Bob Lemmon, at that time general secretary of the Highland Society. The shoe sat in his office until he retired but I have no idea of its whereabouts now.

At that time the Royal Highland Show was the main show in Scotland. Despite this, there were only two competitions, the Heavy Horse Shoemaking and the Heavy Horse Shoeing, so if you wanted to do well, you did not have many opportunities.

I continued my partnership with Jock McKenzie, as we seemed to work together well. We would start practising once a week from the turn of the year and this would increase to three times a week right up to the show in June.

Going back a couple of years before Ingliston, in 1958 we competed at the Highland Show that was held in Ayr. It was not a successful show for me even though I finished in time; I was out with the prizes.

The following year, which was the last time the show would be 'on the road,' it was held in Aberdeen and I managed to get an eighth prize. That may not seem very good but at that time there were about sixty competitors in the senior classes and the prizes went down to ninth.

The Highland Show held in 1962 is well remembered by me as it was at this event I got my first win, in the Heavy Horse Shoemaking where I received the Capewell Gold Medal. This was the first of thirteen top awards I managed to win at the Highland in this competition.

Preparing for the Highland Show by shoeing a
Clydesdale belonging to David Young.

In the 1970s, with the influx of light-legged horses into Scotland, the show organisers started a Hunter Shoemaking competition. This was later to be divided again into a Therapeutic Shoemaking class and a Hunter Shoeing class. This expansion, with the extra two competitions, made for a busy four days. It also enabled me to win over forty first prizes at the Highland Show in fifty years of competing.

I should say that competing at these shows is very much a team effort, with two men, one as the fireman and striker and the other the competitor. The roles are then reversed. It is essential the two work together. For a quarter of a century, Jock and I worked as a team helping each other to the best of our ability, not worrying who won. Our objective was always to try and be first and second. This, of course, did not always work, as the rest of the competitors were trying to do the same.

While the number of competitions increased, the Heavy Horse shoeing class was always the one that attracted most spectators. Everyone wanted to see the big Clydesdales being shod.

The horses waiting to be shod were numbered and the numbers put into a hat. The competitors then had to choose a number from the hat to determine which horse they would shoe.

The tension would then build around the competition area, with lots of thoughts and doubts going through the competitors' minds. Did that horse have good feet? Would it stand still? Has it been shod before with hot shoes? Would it be afraid of the smoke? And would it be twitchy with all the noise and hubbub around?

Although every horse is different, I never made any fuss over the horse I had chosen. Some were more fidgety than others and one or two would try to lean on you as you worked, but moaning about the chosen horse was just an excuse in my opinion.

Jock retired from competing after he started breeding Welsh Ponies. This took up a lot of his time and when he started to show them at the Highland, he decided that to do both was impossible, so I had to look for another partner.

I then worked with Sandy Duff from Macmerry in East Lothian and although I did not know it until years later, there had been a close link between our families several generations earlier.

Sandy was from a long line of farriers/blacksmiths. He served his apprenticeship with his father in Dunfermline before moving to East Saltoun Smiddy, East Lothian, which is in one of the most fertile areas of Scotland. He had been fairly successful at shows, mainly on light horses before we teamed up, so again, this turned into another good partnership. We originally worked together at the Lancashire Show in Blackpool in 1972 when I won the Champion of Champions. For this competition, you had to qualify by having won a major competition before. This was my first venture into England, and I think it was a bit of a surprise that this unknown Scotsman – well, unknown to them anyway – walked away with their major prize.

On that Blackpool expedition, we had our wives with us, Joan and Mairi, and I had made it a week of my holidays. All the English guys were great sports and wanted to take us out for a drink after my victory, but we were booked into a variety show that night. They asked us which theatre we were going to and said they would meet up with us afterwards. Sure enough they were there, and as we came out of the theatre, they hoisted me up on their shoulders and carried me up the Blackpool street.

They stopped two or three taxis to take us to a pub, but it was late and the pubs were closed and all that was open was a strip club. So there we were, about fourteen men, two strippers and Mairi and Joan. Mairi had visions of appearing in the paper the next day or being arrested, but all ended without incident.

Sandy and I competed together successfully for a few years until my son David was old enough to work alongside me. Further proof of the tendency of sons to follow their fathers into the business came when Sandy's son also joined him in the business. Both the Wilson and Duff families now have another generation of farriers at work, and Sandy and I both have grandchildren shoeing horses. As we travelled and competed, we talked of our own forefathers and it was then I found out his great grandfather and grandfather had taken over Hazelton smiddy in 1876 and worked there for twenty-two years. Hazelton is only three or four miles from Kilmany and I am sure my grandfather would have known the Duffs.

One year in my Highland Show competing career particularly stands out, and that was 1984, as my son David and I won all the cups between us. David won the apprentice cup and I won all the senior trophies. His success, which came in his third year of competition at the Highland, was against twelve apprentices. This shows the increased level of interest and competition in farrier work nowadays.

Sometimes, as I think back over the people I have competed against over the years, it seems there were more characters amongst the guys back then, but maybe that is just the musings and rose-tinted memories of an old man.

With my son David after a successful
Highland Show in 1992.

51

Prize winners with sponsors outside the Highland Show
headquarters after the presentation in 1992.

Any discussion of characters would have to include the Martins
from Closeburn near Thornhill in Dumfriesshire. They again had
a long-established blacksmith's business going back two or three
generations. Two of the Martin sons, Edward and Murray, were
farriers and blacksmiths, and competed, with their father chapping for
them, or hammering as it is more politely called. When this family
team competed, they worked at breakneck speed, with father Ed, who
was a gruff kind of guy, still encouraging them to work 'faster, faster'
when it seemed impossible to go any faster. But when the bell went
for finishing the round, it was well done to each other and off they
would go for a pint.

They were good smiths and always featured on the prize list.
Edward was also a very good wrought-iron worker and gate-maker
and won many prizes over the years. The story is told about when
Edward and Murray were working in their smiddy in two fires, with
one making one piece, then passing it over to the other to finish it.
A young man came in for an interview for a job. Edward looked up
momentarily and said, 'Just wait a minute until we finish,' and went
back to the job in hand with sweat and hot iron flying all around.
Eventually the brothers finished their work and said, 'Now lad, we

believe you are looking for a job.' The young man looked up at the sweat-streaked questioner and then across to his equally perspiring brother and replied, 'Not now I'm not,' and walked out the door, never to be seen again.

Another blacksmithing family were the Stephen brothers from the Montrose area: Willie, Jim and Ralph. Willie had his smiddy in Montrose, Jim was at Northwaterbridge and I am not sure about Ralph. They were very tall and thin, and I can remember Jim being well over six foot tall. They were all very good craftsmen and featured well up in the prize lists, especially Willie, or Wull, as he was known. He was an excellent shoemaker and won quite a few gold medals.

Then there was Alex Redford from Glendoick. He had a long red beard like Rob Roy. He was a very good horseshoer, particularly of horses with bad feet. Proving that blacksmiths often followed other members of their families into the job, Alex was also one of three brothers who were all blacksmiths and competed at the shows. In addition to Alex, there was Jack from Kinrossie and Geordie who worked in Broughty Ferry.

The lads most local to me were Jack Scott and Maurice Smith from Cupar. Jack was a very good gate-maker as well as a farrier and went on to be farrier tutor at Elmwood College in Cupar. Jack and Maurice used to shout at each other all the time when competing, much to the amusement of the spectators.

Maurice used to describe Wilson and McKenzie as an 'odd pair of buggers' because we did not speak to each other when we competed. We did not have to, as we knew exactly what each other was going to do.

The Highland Show always employed a chief steward to look after and help run the horseshoeing competition. My first memory was of a Mr Hume, who at that time was employed in a solicitor's office, so his work at the Highland must have been a complete contrast. He is the only steward I knew who everyone called Mr, as he was such a gentleman. No one thought of calling him by his name, which was Archie.

He was followed by Ramsay Blair, a blacksmith from Currie. As a former competitor himself he knew the ropes and was often able to sort out problems before they became problems. When he retired, the chief steward's responsibilities passed to Tom Buchanan, who worked at the Longannet power station in Fife. I took over in 1994 until I retired in 2006.

The chief steward's responsibilities include making the draw for the rounds as well as organising the supply of steel and coal. It also includes

Discussing the judging with Ken Cunningham
and Archie Hume.

looking after the judges. Some of them like to keep themselves to themselves prior to the competition, but most enjoy a pre-competition dram and sometimes two before they start their work.

For hospitality, we had a room at the back of the stand, where cups of tea and biscuits were provided for friends and family members. It was a very popular meeting place for visitors and many came to rest their weary legs after trailing around the showground. I have been told we blacksmiths had a very popular lady in charge of this facility but Mairi always claimed that she was happy to look after it as I was always otherwise occupied.

As chief steward, I also had to keep and make sure the result sheets were correct and the prize tickets were ready to dish out when the time came. The chief steward has two or three helpers to see to the fires and generally keep the workshop floor tidy. None of the duties are too onerous, but woe betide a chief steward if any part of the organisation fails.

The old shoeing stand with its canvas tent roof and railway-sleeper floor was taken down in the 1990s and we were allocated the old sheep-shearing building as our new venue for the competition. I was, by this time, chief steward, so it was left to me to get it in order.

Originally there had been four fires, which were made by Houston's of Cupar. Each of them came complete with electric motors. When we made the move, I built four new double fires but still used the original electric blowers. We also built a new extractor system to draw away the smoke from the chimneys as this had been an occasional problem in the past. Once those improvements had been made, the new, or new to us, facility was a great building. It was totally roofed and it had a superb stand for the spectators, where they could see all the action.

Another attraction over the years at the shoeing stand was the wrought-iron gate competition. I remember at Dundee Highland Show in 1957 when there were about twenty-five to thirty gates entered and at that time there was no electric or gas welding allowed. All the entries had to be riveted or forge welded.

These gates were all made at home prior to the show. The competitors always planned make them in the winter when they were quiet, but this never happened and there was always a last-minute rush the night before the show.

One year I was through at the show the day before it opened and some of the gates entered for the competition were on display. I thought the standard was not very high. I had entered a gate on the schedule but had not had time to make one. When I arrived home I said to Mairi, 'I think I'll take your mum's gate off its hinges at her house and enter it in the Highland.' I had made this gate and entered it in the show two years before, where it won third prize. Mairi's mum and dad were on holiday and, as I eased it off its hinges, I think the neighbours thought I was stealing the gate. I brought it home where I burned the paint off with the oxyacetylene burner. Then I resprayed it and took it through at six o' clock on the morning of the show. I won first prize.

Times changed and the wrought-iron class attracted fewer and fewer entries. It was agreed that it would be permissible to allow electric-welded gates, mainly to keep the cost down, as it was far quicker to work like that. This boosted the entries for a year or two but eventually the entries fell away again and the competition was ended in 2006.

I continued to be chief steward and ran the horseshoeing competition until 2006. Between competing and officiating, this gave me fifty years of continuous involvement with the Royal Highland Show. To mark my half century, the show directors invited Mairi and me to lunch and presented me not with a horse being shod, but

Now inspecting.

with a Border Fine Art ornament of a Highland calf, which graces the mantelpiece of our home to this day.

Competing at the Highland provided fifty years of enjoyment I will never forget.

Chapter 7

Our Own Business

AFTER having worked at Jock McKenzie's smiddy at Ayton for quite a number of years, I felt it was time for me and Mairi to branch out on our own. I think it was always in my blood to be my own boss.

Hazelton smiddy was the first place we looked at, but decided it was too close to the river Tay. It lies in a wonderful location with beautiful views of the river, but I knew that to have a chance of running a successful business it was better to have a full circle as a catchment area and not, as would have been the case at Hazelton, only a semi-circle of potential customers. Another major reason we scored it off our 'possible list' was that Jock already had most of the customers in that area.

We also looked at the old family base at Kilmany. The smiddy there might have been adequate in the days of horsepower, but it was too small to cope with farmers coming in with tractors and machinery for repairs and there was no room for expansion.

Then we heard about Balmullo smiddy. It had been empty for about six months, and we decided to investigate a bit further. The smiddy was sublet by neighbouring farmer, David Bell, of Pusk Farm, Leuchars. I made an appointment to see him, and his first question was, 'Can you shoe horses?' He was one of the last farmers in the area to continue to work with horses. At that time, he still worked most of his land with his big Clydesdales, although, in a concession to the modern world, he did have one tractor. I told him I could shoe horses, and that was the end of the interview. It was the only requirement he needed. The rent was six pounds per year, which was well within our budget.

I took Mairi along to see if the house would be suitable for our three girls, a dog, a cat, and, of course, had enough space for my pigeon loft. Some papering and painting needed to be done, but apart from that it was perfect. Outside the smiddy, there was plenty room for customers to drop off their broken machinery, and apart from laying some concrete on parts of the floor, I was ready to begin in business.

We moved from Ayton on 28 November 1962 and I started work on 1 December. Financially I think we had about fifty pounds between us and most of that was from Mairi's mum. I bought some bits and pieces that were left by the last blacksmith and borrowed a welder from Jock.

Dave Lang, son of one of the local farmers, took me round all the farms in the area and introduced me to his neighbours. There were also a number of businesses nearby that could provide work for a keen young blacksmith. The most famous one is the Redstone quarry, which with its orange red scar in the hill can be seen by every visitor to St Andrew's, whether they be golfer or university student.

There was also a Bluestone quarry, which although it is now closed down, was still working at that time. Within a mile of the Balmullo smiddy, a sand and gravel quarry is still in operation.

That first year, we had a very frosty winter and no ploughing was carried out until almost the middle of March. This was bad news, as ploughing time always used to be a busy time for local blacksmiths, with embarrassed workers coming in with bent and twisted ploughs after hitting some hidden boulder. Either that or it was angry farmers coming in needing more, in their words, 'bl★★dy plough metal'.

With the late season not helping us, we were beginning to wonder if we had done the right thing by moving away from Ayton and the security it provided. However, it was only a matter of time before business improved and the spring work on the farms got underway.

Mairi sent out the first accounts promptly and thankfully they were all paid very quickly. One farmer, whose bill came to one pound and thirteen shillings (£1.65) for the month of December, gave us a cheque for fifty pounds to credit his account. He said he knew these early days were when we really needed the money and he would just work off his credit. We really appreciated this gesture of kindness. It was over a year until we had to charge him for anything.

Another who was to help establish the business in the early days was Major Sir William Anstruther-Gray from Kilmany House. He was later to become Lord Kilmany. He asked me to take on the task of shoeing his racehorses, at a cost of one pound and eighteen shillings (£1.90) for four new shoes, refits for twelve shillings and sixpence (63p) and we charged five shillings (25p) for the mileage, which entailed a round trip of eight miles. As I travelled over to his stables one day I reckoned the fees I was charging were not much more than my father had done thirty years before. There was, however, a little cachet for me as blacksmith, as I could claim to be looking after the Kilmany racing stables, which were the most northerly in the country at that time.

As time went by, the business settled down. We had regular farm customers and while they had initially moved to dealing with bigger machinery companies from whom they bought their tractors and other machines, they soon found out that their local smith was not as expensive as they had thought he was, and he was much more available.

As time wore on, the equipment on farms grew bigger and bigger, with larger tractors needing larger ploughs and machinery. At the same time, combines took over from binders and balers took over from loose hay and straw stacks. All this machinery was good news for the local blacksmith, especially in parts of the country where there were either a lot of stones or rock heads in the fields. A third bonus came with poor tractor drivers. Whether physical or human, those factors meant more breakdowns for the blacksmith to sort out. For some farms with rocky ground, there was almost a daily visit to the smiddy with their bent ploughs. Fixing these is an easy job nowadays with a power press, and sheer brute force can be used to straighten up bent machinery, but back when I started we had to heat the plough beams in the fire and untwist them over the anvil with the sledge hammer and then retemper them by cooling them in the water tank slowly. If this was not done properly there was a danger the metal could be made too brittle and the next time it hit a rock it would break. Cue a return visit to the smiddy.

There were other changes in farm machinery that increased the traffic to and from the smiddy. Old cart wheels with their steel rims were now obsolete and every piece of equipment either had rubber

Fitting new metal rims to an old cart wheel.

tyres or was carried on the three-point linkage of the tractor. I could not tell you how many old machines were given a new lease of life with a conversion from the old horse shafts to the three-point linkage, but it must have been hundreds.

In the mid 1970s, I became heavily involved in another revolution in farming. Up until that point, potatoes were always planted in ridges. The harvesting of that ridge saw people picking out the potatoes from among the clods and stones. On a good day a hand picker could gather two tonnes of potatoes. Then someone thought, what if there were no stones or clods to sort out? The potatoes could be harvested by machinery, and the machines could and now do harvest hundreds of tonnes every day with no hand labour.

The race was on to build a de-stoning machine to go through the ridges before the potatoes were planted. I was asked to make ten machines under contract for one of the innovators, Will Scorgie.

His design was for a single-row machine driven with hydraulic motors. The webs separated the soil and the stones, with the former forming a stone-free drill. At harvest time, if the job had been done right, with an elevator the potato digger could put the potatoes straight into a trailer.

These early model Scorgie machines, although very efficient, were very slow, and the next year, I decided to invent one myself. It was a two-row trailed machine that was driven by the power take-off from the tractor. The prototype was made and tried in the month of November. It almost worked, but required some modifications, which were carried out. Such was the surge of enthusiasm for de-stoning machines that one of the local machinery dealers took orders for about twenty-five of my design.

We started making them on the second day in January. To have started on New Year's Day in Scotland would have caused quite a reaction as this has always been a traditional holiday. Unlike in England, where Christmas Day is sacrosanct, New Year's Day is the holiday for working people in Scotland. In fact, at the start of my working life, 25 December was a working day.

From the second day of the year right through to the end of April, Alan Fairlie, who was employed by me at that time, and I worked every day of the week and every night.

By the end of April, we had made fifteen machines and we were so tired we were only going at half speed. I vowed there and then that I would never work like that again and that even if we were busy we would take every second weekend off.

Making all those machines in our old smiddy underlined how cramped the building was, or to put it another way, the machinery we were dealing with was bigger but our premises had remained the same size for the best part of the century. We decided we had to expand into a bigger building.

Plans were drawn up and submitted to the local authority as well as to our factor, as we were still working on a year-to-year lease at that time. After a great deal of discussion, we managed to agree on a twenty-year lease. Like many farm tenants, we took the gamble and built our workshop on the understanding that if anything happened to me, the workshop would revert to the estate.

As part of our negotiations, we had tried to buy the property, but were unsuccessful at that time. In later years, after the landlord died we were given the opportunity to buy the house, the old smiddy and the land the workshop was built on. We took the plunge into ownership.

With bigger premises and with a change in ownership of the buildings we turned our minds back to work. Our de-stoning machines, which we called Kingdom Separators, after their creation in the Kingdom of Fife, had not worked as well as we had hoped. We decided to take them back to carry out minor modifications to help their performance.

We found it so much easier working in the larger premises, and although we did not laugh much at the time, we recalled the problems of always having to watch out for tripping over bits of machinery in our previous cramped smiddy. The increased space made it much easier to carry out our work, and all in all it was a very satisfying time as the modified de-stoners were much more efficient and were also pleasing to the eye.

All my own work: the Kingdom de-stoner.

Although they now worked very well, they were made for single-row harvesters. As such, our two-row models were slightly ahead of their time. However, one of the international potato machinery manufacturers moved to two-row harvesting and the same company started producing two-row de-stoners that had far more web capacity than our machines. As a result they could cover a bigger acreage per hour or per day than ours. Within three years of being invented, our Kingdom Separators were considered to be out of date as the new de-stoners were now far bigger than we could manufacture. That marked the end of our involvement in producing machinery for potato producers.

After looking around for another business opportunity, our next venture was to make bulk loaders for trucks. We received an order for two from a local haulage contractor who could see that there was a shift towards bulk handling of animal feed. The bulk bodies were made with steel frames, wooden sides and an endless conveyor belt up the middle of the floor to empty the feedstuff. These bulkers, as they were known, were going to be used for transporting and handling bulk maize into a local distillery.

Describing what the bulker should do was the easy bit. Getting it to do as it should was more difficult as there was a problem trying to keep the feed maize from jamming under the belt. On two occasions we

Constructing a new shed for a customer.

The satisfaction of completing building a shed.

had to shovel out ten tons of maize through a small one-foot-square door at the back. It was not a very easy job and there were a few frayed tempers. Eventually, the solution was found as we overcame the problem with rubber strips pressurised down on the main belt. Again we were under pressure to deliver these bodies to a tight time limit, and in scenes reminiscent of making the de-stoners, this involved us having to work night shifts. The local joiner, Bill Morrison, was pulled in to do all the woodwork on the bulkers and he and I and my sole employee were being fed by Mairi in the workshop to ensure we lost no time travelling home – approximately twenty yards each way – to eat. Sometimes, sitting down to have our meals, we were unsure if it was supper or breakfast at the times we came in.

In hindsight I think we should have continued making these bulkers, but I always had the feeling that the local smithy was there to service the farming community.

This was a big mistake, however, for farmers were starting to buy their own welders and machinery was becoming much more sophisticated and complicated.

Our next move was to enter the industrial market, which in our case meant supplying the local Ministry of Defence RAF base at Leuchars. We won the contract to supply steel, which was mainly used for fabrication or repair work.

Because it was a top defence base, security at the camp was very high and we all had to have clearance documents complete with passes containing our photos, something a bit out of the normal run of things for a village blacksmith. Such was the high level of security at the base that the smiddy truck with all our equipment also had to have a pass.

The whole security process was very time consuming, especially if something had to be welded at the bomb dump or where the explosives were stored. In these cases, a 'hot work' permit had to be issued and a fire engine had to be on hand. Sometimes getting all the paperwork and security in place took longer than doing the job.

There were now four people working in the business and they were kept very busy. One of my everlasting memories was making steel pipes that had to be pushed through an existing concrete drain that ran right underneath the main runway. This drain took the water from a small stream and into the nearby Motray estuary. The pipe was in three-metre sections and it was 860 millimetres in diameter. To get the pipe in place, it was pushed by hydraulics through the drain, which was about one hundred yards long. After it had been inserted, I had to crawl up inside the pipe on a converted skateboard in order to bore holes for drains. All the time I was working, the pipe had six inches of water running through it, so to stop me from getting soaked, I wore a wetsuit. I remember on one occasion I was up the pipe and felt the water rising. Out the pipe I scrambled, and found the young

Bulk tanks constructed in the smiddy.

man who was supposed to keep a safety check on me had fallen asleep. Meanwhile engineers downstream had dammed the water as part of another project and had forgotten about me. The young man was not a very popular chap that day, I can tell you. This job lasted for three weeks and I was extremely glad when it ended.

We were also kept very busy with Fife Council Road Works department, who wanted us to service their snow ploughs and get them ready for action in the winter. One year, when there had been some very bad snow storms, there were snow ploughs queued up outside the workshop waiting to be repaired. With the phone ringing from their bosses asking how soon they could be in action again, my employees and I had to give them top priority. Winter normally being a quiet time for farm work, this was a valuable contract, as it kept the smiddy busy.

So far, I have not mentioned the people who worked for me over my forty years at Balmullo. It is a well-known fact that for small businesses to be successful, everyone has to pull together in the same direction. I reckon I was fortunate in the men who worked for me, and I did not go the lengths of Jock McKenzie who, when taking on a new apprentice, always asked to meet a new employee's parents. 'You have to make sure the breeding is right,' he used to say in justification.

As previously mentioned, my first employee was Alan Fairlie. Alan had been there when we were in the old smiddy in the de-stoning machinery era. In the winter time, when the snow came down, we would go into the building in the morning and find all the machines covered in snow. After quite a number of years, Alan left to work as a mechanic at the Redstone quarry, where he eventually became the manager.

Next I employed Robin Steven. Robin had been a farmer but wanted to go to Canada and had been offered a job as a farm mechanic. He came and worked for a few weeks to learn welding and other blacksmith skills before emigrating. However, things did not work out as expected in Canada, so he and his wife and family came back to Scotland. Robin returned to the smiddy and worked with me until I retired.

He was such a reliable chap and came down the road to the smiddy at ten minutes to eight o'clock every morning. This was the complete opposite of my next apprentice Calum MacPherson. He was always late. I would hear his motorbike two miles away roaring along the road at ten minutes past eight. But he became a very talented worker and now runs his own very successful business.

My first farrier apprentice was Andrew Crow, who came from Linlithgow. Both of his parents were teachers and I recall when he came through for his interview, his mother said Andrew must be 'full of work as he has never done any so far in his life'. Andrew's original idea was that a blacksmith would sit under the spreading chestnut tree smoking a pipe. It took a while, but he eventually turned out to be an excellent farrier.

As the business grew, I felt I needed someone to take a bit of the pressure away and give me some free time. I was fortunate enough to get Leslie Spence, who had worked for Houston's of Cupar. He had a lot of knowledge and was able to read drawings and diagrams and translate them into what actually had to be done. Les became my workshop foreman and was also there until I retired.

Mairi and I had actually been increasing our own domestic workforce with the arrival in 1965 of our son David. After three daughters, this was an event that I celebrated by going round Balmullo – which was much smaller in those days – peeping the horn of my van and telling anyone who was out and about, 'We've got a son.'

When David was about four years old, Bill Clark came to work with me. Bill had a vast knowledge of all blacksmithing. David was very fond of Bill and the two of them used to bake potatoes in the smiddy fire. Not a lot of profit was being made but it kept David out of Mairi's hair while she got on with the office work. Bill eventually had to retire due to ill health. He would have been an excellent man from whom to learn the trade.

Alex Cooper joined the team for a short period of time. Alex came from Shetland and it took a wee while to understand the accent. In fact I am not sure if I ever did get the lilt.

In 1982, our son David left school and decided he wanted to become a farrier. I had almost given up shoeing at that time, having crashed a car a few years before and hurt my back. By now I was on the mend, though, so I went back to fulltime farriery in order to train David. The four years of his apprenticeship went by very quickly and he was soon qualified. I wanted to get back into the workshop, so he went off and started his own business.

In 1987, after we came back from Calgary, David decided to go over to America and work for six months with friends we had met at the world championships. It was the right time in his life to do this, but he found that shoeing horses in a temperature of over ninety degrees and high humidity was not much fun. He came back home and eventually joined the family firm again, this time as an engineer fabricator. He was a very good one but I think the farrier bug was always there. Not long after, he started his own business for a second time and has never looked back. Now his own son Josh is a qualified farrier and is working with his dad.

Over the years, we did a wide variety of work. I can remember not too long ago we had four cart wheels on which we had to put rims. By this time, we did not have a double fire in the smiddy large enough to take the rims or the flat plate that always used to lie outside smiddy doors. I think perhaps it had been sold for scrap, as I never imagined it would be required again.

We put the four rims outside with bales of straw and wood around them and heated them all together. We blocked up the wheels with pieces of steel, and then we were ready. Young David, Calum and I worked together, sweat pouring off us, lifting and turning the whole time. The first rim on top worked well and we got it on the wheel and finished. The next two rims got jammed into each other and became all twisted. We had to cool them, then straighten them out and start again but we made it in the end. It was a good team effort.

Another job we did was to assemble a new stone crusher at the Redstone quarry. The main parts for the crusher came from France and a French engineer had been sent over to supervise the installation. This was quite a task, especially with a slight language barrier. I remember trying to fit a long bolt about two feet long by two inches in diameter. Suddenly, the bolt slipped and it came down on my thumb. There was blood everywhere. The Frenchman, looking quite unconcerned, said that in Arabia, when they had finished erecting a crusher, they used to kill a goat and then sprinkle its blood on the crusher for good luck. He remarked, as I hopped about holding my bloody finger, that they would not have to do that here as there was enough blood already.

Sometimes at weekends when all the men were off, the workshop would be empty on a Saturday afternoon. I was often out dealing with combine breakdowns or away at farriery competitions when an irate farmer would rush in with something that needed welding immediately. Seeing there was no one else available, Mairi decided that she needed to be able to weld. This was arranged through the Scottish Rural Development Department, which organised training courses. The welding instructor arrived, and after a few lessons, Mairi was able to weld. She did not really get to use this skill to a great extent. For instance, a few weeks after completing the course, a tractor driver came in with a broken dung spreader. Mairi was in charge and said, 'Just take it into the workshop and I'll soon weld it.' The man looked at her and said, 'It's all right, Mrs, I'm not that desperate. I'll bring it back on Monday morning.'

After forty years of running our own business, the pace was beginning to tell, according to Mairi, who often saw her husband coming home from work looking tired and worn out. I was over sixty years old in

End of an era at the dispersal sale at the smiddy.

2000 when we made the decision to sell up. To this day I am not sure if we should have carried on for a few more years or not. Two issues are clear, though. The first was that the clientele of the business had changed. No longer did the majority of the work come from farms: the new customers were local businesses that needed skilled welders. The second issue was that there was plenty of work, but having too much to do can be more difficult to cope with than not having enough.

We held a roup, or sale, of the equipment in the smiddy, with customers, clients and curious neighbours crowding the yard during the proceedings. Standing among the throng, I watched the auctioneer selling the tools and equipment I had used over the past four decades. It was the end of an era.

Chapter 8

Official Duties

NORMALLY after a shoeing competition, we blacksmiths sit around and banter with each other as the judges get down to their task of sorting out who has done the best job on the day. Our talk is mostly local gossip on how business is going or how is old so and so whom we have not seen since last year. The chat is free and easy as we have been friends, colleagues and competitors for years.

All of which made me wonder what Mairi and I would be able to talk about at the grandly titled Livery Banquet to which we had been invited at the Lord Mayor of London's Mansion House; not just invited but, as honoured guests, we were to be seated at the top table.

We were pretty sure that the other guests would not be interested in local gossip or even the fact that the price of shoeing horses had not risen in line with inflation in recent years, so what would we talk about between the soup and the steak, without even thinking as far ahead as the pudding?

However as President of the National Association of Blacksmiths, Farriers and Agricultural Engineers, this banquet was one of the many social functions I had to attend.

For those who have not been to Mansion House, it is an incredibly imposing building just across the road from the Bank of England, right in the centre of the City of London. It was definitely a case of putting on my best bib and tucker, so the Wilson tartan kilt was brought out and, with Mairi in a lovely ballgown, we proceeded from our hotel to the banquet.

I had been told to wear my chain of office and initially thought of putting it on as we dressed in the hotel, but knowing that it had just been valued at eleven thousand pounds and we had a bit to walk along the streets of London, I just tucked it into my kilt sporran. As Mairi remarked, 'That is the most money that has ever been in there.' Jumping forward in my story, when it came to squaring up for the luxurious hotel in which we stayed during the visit I actually thought we had bought the hotel, instead of just having a room for the night.

We could not see another kilted person as we entered the reception area of Mansion House. This was called the Salon, which I found quite funny as on our trips to America we often ended up in saloons and they were much less grand.

Mairi and I pictured after I'd been installed as President.

What we could see were lots and lots of people with colourful costumes and red ermine-trimmed robes. When we looked at the seating plan we saw that we were surrounded by Aldermen, Ambassadors, Sheriffs, chaplains and Masters of the various Companies, not to mention the Lord and Lady Mayoress at the top table. However, when the toastmaster Jamie Wallis announced the top table, he not only gave me my title as President of the National Association of Farriers, Blacksmiths and Agricultural Engineers, but added BEM, FWCF and AWCB after my name. The explanation for those awards will come later.

The Master of the Worshipful Company of Farriers and chairman for the evening, Dr John Garnham, soon put us at ease and introduced us to the Lord Mayor and the Lady Mayoress. On finding out my background was working with horses, the Lady Mayoress told us she kept a donkey at home. From then on, even although I have never shod a donkey in my life, we had some common ground and therefore no worries about what to talk about.

What may be more difficult for people to believe is that when we, blacksmiths, are in the post-competition lull while we wait for the judges to make their decisions, my friends do not believe I talked about donkeys with the Lady Mayoress of London.

To tell the truth, I was still quite overawed by the occasion, with all the pomp and ceremony that included a string quintet playing in a box up in the balcony of the main hall. Not, I thought, the sort of thing that happens much in Balmullo.

The decor and architecture of Mansion House was quite amazing even if we did not see many of the famous paintings and we only saw a fraction of what I was told was one the largest collections of gold and silver plate in the world.

Our next visit to Mansion House was the following year, as National Association presidents serve two years in office. This time we were a little better prepared for what we were about to receive. We also had our Scottish friends there, Jim and Shona Ferrie, who spoke our language.

Again we were at the top table and again there was live music but this time it was played by a quintet from the Blues and Royals so it was a case of more military tunes and quite different.

Mairi and I were more relaxed the second time around and we enjoyed it tremendously, but we both keep our feet on the ground and were not carried away with all the pomp.

During times like those, I sometimes wondered how I had ended up at what might be considered the top end of the profession. The only answer I could find was that, just like many others roads I have travelled in my life, I started at the bottom.

In my case, in the middle of the 1950s in Scotland, very few farriers had any written qualifications. They were all accomplished time-served horseshoers but there were no pieces of paper on the wall to confirm their abilities. I could see we were moving into an era where paper qualifications were becoming essential.

The Worshipful Company of Farriers wanted to set up a register of farriers and they sent an expert up from England to go round all the local blacksmiths to train them, mainly on the theory, as well as helping with the practical side when necessary.

When the expert came to our part of the world, all the farriers, including myself, went to Dunfermline to the Co-operative workshops. There we were examined and interviewed on our skills.

The practical examination involved shoeing one front foot and one hind foot of a draught horse. This was followed by questions on the horse's leg, bones and hoof structure.

Most people attending the course passed the examination. This was a tribute to the traditional system of master blacksmith and apprentice. In due course, we all received certificates confirming we were Registered Shoeing Smiths (RSS). These were the first letters I had after my name, although in my early days as an apprentice, I sometimes had adjectives put in front of my name when I made a mistake.

As can be imagined when horses were the main power source in business, those who looked after their feet were valued members of the community. Back in July 1691, less than three decades after the Great Fire swept through London, the Worshipful Company of Farriers petitioned the Court of Aldermen to become one of the Liveried Companies of the City of London, which explains why Mairi and I were swanking in Mansion House.

But the history of horseshoeing in London goes much further back, with the Mayor of London in 1356 summoning the farriers in the city to deal with offences and damages by 'people not wise therein who kept forges and meddled with practices they did not understand'. At that time, the Mayor ordered the choosing of two wardens to oversee the trade.

One of the main roles of the Livery Company was to ensure that apprentices were properly trained in the skills of shoeing horses, and in 1975, a bill was put through Parliament that stated that all farriers in England, Wales and Scotland, with the exception of the Highlands and Islands, were to be registered.

When this was introduced it had four parts. Part one was for farriers who had already passed their RSS exam. Part two was mainly for farriers who had shod for many years but held no qualifications. Part three was for horse owners who shod their own horses, and part four was for anyone who was left out. In years to come, with natural wastage, only part one was left.

Those starting off in the trade today, both boys and girls, and there are quite a few girls, now have to do a four-year apprenticeship with an approved training farrier followed by twenty-one weeks at college. Providing they come through successfully, they will be awarded their diploma and will then be placed on the register. Ever since the introduction of the Act, it has been a civil offence to shoe horses without being registered.

I mention this as I spent fifteen years as a fully-fledged examiner. During that time I travelled to the various colleges throughout Britain offering training in becoming a farrier. These places of learning included the agricultural colleges in Hereford, Warwick, Myrescough (Lancashire), Oatridge (West Lothian) and Enniskillen in Northern Ireland.

My stint as an examiner only came after I sat other exams to prove my prowess as a farrier. First of all I sat my Associate exam in 1975. This was mainly therapeutic shoemaking but also included a written question paper on the theory. Never having been much of a student in my schoolboy days, I was pleased to pass this with Honours and was then an Associate of the Worshipful Company of Farriers (AWCF), not forgetting the Hons after the initials.

Two years after that exam I sat my Fellowship, which was much more theory related. The first exercise was to write a three-thousand-word essay on the principles and practices of horseshoeing. I also had to give a lecture to a veterinarian and two farrier examiners who were both already Fellows. I worried that this would not be easy and so was pleasantly surprised when I realised they understood what I was talking about.

It was only after going through those exams that I was invited to become an examiner for the Worshipful Company. At first I turned the invitation down, as there was so much work to do at home. It just was not the right time for me. A few years later, when I had more help in the workshop, I accepted the post.

So far, I have not explained my role in the National Association of Farriers, Blacksmiths and Agricultural Engineers. The National Association started in 1905, although smaller branches had been formed before this. Representatives from these branches were called to a meeting in Birmingham and from that meeting the foundations of the National Association were laid.

In the post World War One years, when horses were still a major force in transportation and on farms, the membership of the National Association had soared to over fifteen thousand.

The 1920s, with the country in the grip of a deep economic depression, was also the first time the Association flexed its muscle at local and national level. In areas all around the country, local blacksmiths banded together to resist any fall in the price of shoeing horses.

Angry meetings with farmers who were themselves facing hefty reductions in the prices they were getting for their produce saw the Association try to establish a minimum price for shoeing a horse. This attempt to put a base in the market failed, with local blacksmiths being threatened with a loss of trade if they did not reduce their prices.

While that attempt by the Association to help its membership failed, it was more successful with a sickness, accident and death benefit system that it put in place to help members who were struggling to survive financially if they had an accident. Thus the widow of a member who had died would benefit from the Association. This continued until 1971, when it was agreed that such a national insurance scheme was no longer necessary.

I joined the Association in 1962 when we moved to Balmullo and started my own business. I was affiliated to the East Fife and Kirkcaldy

Branch, which met quarterly and had around twenty members. The topics discussed would be mainly horseshoeing, the price of steel, wages and other issues affecting our businesses. There was a price list out at that time, which was a good guide for me to follow, having just gone into business on my own. This price list later became illegal after the government passed legislation outlawing price fixing.

For my own part, I attended my first National annual meeting in Dunblane in 1970. At that time it came to Scotland every seven years and there were delegates attending from all over the UK.

It was quite an occasion for Mairi and me, as we had not been to anything like that before. There was a full day of business and discussions with new committees being formed and the issues of the day being debated. It was the first time I had really realised that, up and down the country, blacksmiths and farriers were facing similar problems.

Some years later, I became a delegate for the East Fife and Kirkcaldy Branch. There were four districts, North East Scotland, North West, South East and South West, all with delegates attending meetings in Edinburgh. The district was responsible for choosing the judges for the Highland Show. Judges would be suggested from alternate districts each year.

As horses ceased to be a major supplier of power on farms, membership decreased and Scotland became one district. Mairi, who had been our branch secretary for a number of years, took over the position of district secretary, a post she held until I finished my term as President.

In 1989 I was voted onto the Executive Committee of the National Association. Little did I know then that I would be driving up and down to Stoneleigh, Warwickshire, to the head office, for the next thirteen years, and that I would be doing this round trip of more than six hundred miles at least five or six times a year.

By 1993 my rise up the official ladder continued when I was voted Vice President. This gave me a real insight into the working of a national organisation, as the government was trying to deregulate the Farriers Registration Act. I am glad this proposal was defeated.

After two years on the second-top rung of the organisation, I was elected President in 1995. It was a special day in my life. Who would believe that someone from the small village of Kilmany would become the National President of the Farriers Association?

At the dinner that evening, the main address, which was absolutely brilliant, was given by Lord Tonypandy, former Speaker of the House of Commons. Mairi then had to make a speech in response to the toast to the ladies.

Presenting Lord Tonypandy with a
handmade letter opener.

Always having been good at composing poetry, Mairi recited a very
well-rehearsed poem she had written. The two verses below give an
idea of her words, which ensured she received a standing ovation.

> In moments of reflection,
> when I look back upon my life.
> I had no recollection,
> I'd be a farrier's wife!
>
> If you should roam the whole wide world,
> no better will you meet,
> than that faithful band of farriers
> who tend the horses' feet.

I was very proud and emotional to have my family there: our three
daughters, along with their husbands, and our son David, his wife and
two children were all dressed up in their finery for the occasion. I
would like to think they were equally proud to see me receiving my

chain of office and their mum being presented with the President's Lady's Brooch.

For my part, my main thought was to get through without any mishaps, and by the end of the night I was relieved that the first big event of my presidency had gone well.

Even though I had been to many executive meetings, I was worried about chairing the main committee. However, some of the old hands still on the committee kept me pointed in the right direction.

Every president over the years has had his own project or problem. In my case it was to move our Association head office to a new site in the Royal Showground in Stoneleigh, Warwickshire.

Although the Association had acquired a building from the Royal Show committee, who owned the whole showground, major work was still to be done. New fires were made for the competitions and a new balcony was put up and erected with railings onto an external staircase.

The new building was double storey, which was a great asset to us as upstairs we had a meeting room, which was named the President's room. This included all the photographs of past presidents as well as a very large boardroom table, which was a beautiful piece of furniture.

The Princess Royal after opening the new forge premises at Stoneleigh.

The Forge all decked out with national flags
before the international competition.

There was also a canteen, with a door leading out onto the balcony, the external stair being used as a fire escape.

I made the external railings and stairs at my own smiddy in Balmullo and transported them down to Stoneleigh with my car and trailer. It was quite an adventure, the load being very much overweight. I had one or two exciting moments on the journey, trying not to exceed fifty miles per hour, as I soon found out that the trailer would start to swing about alarmingly if this speed limit was topped. However, the journey was made and the next day the staircase was erected. It was a big task with many helpers along the way, but well worth all the effort.

The office of the new premises was situated downstairs along with the display room, toilets and the shoeing stand complete with the necessary fires.

The Forge, as it is known, was officially opened by the Princess Royal in 1995. About one hour before the Princess was due to arrive, her bodyguards came in to check over the building along with their sniffer dogs. Unfortunately one of the young farriers had been eating a fish supper and the dogs spent more time trying to get some battered fish and chips rather than look for explosives or whatever else they were supposed to be looking for.

As President, I had the pleasure of escorting the Princess around the building. It was a very proud moment, as well as nerve racking, but she was very knowledgeable regarding the farriers, as she had been a past Master of the Worshipful Company. I can confirm she is also very good at putting people at ease.

Another one of the many privileges of being President was to be invited over to the American Farriers Convention. Again this was a totally new experience for me with four or five hundred farriers from all over the world in attendance. My first Convention was held in Lexington, Kentucky, and as well as representing the British Association, I also competed in the farrier competitions.

The next year we were invited again to the Convention, which this time was held in Lubbock, Texas. Mairi and I flew into Kansas and stayed with our friends Ed and Michelle Zook for a few days. We then hired a car and drove south. I don't know how far it was, but I drove for as long as the tank of petrol lasted and then Ed did the same. We arrived in Lubbock in the evening as the sun was setting in the Texan sky. It was spectacular.

Back on the home front, another of my presidential duties was to oversee the international competitions that were held annually at Stoneleigh. These Internationals had been held since 1979. Gradually the numbers competing increased as the years went by. Earlier I had competed for Scotland in many of those competitions, as has already been recorded.

Some years, teams from more than a dozen countries came to compete. These teams consisted of four farriers. They first competed as individuals and then they teamed up with their compatriots in the second half of the competition. The latter competition was most exciting and had more prestige. Success in this competition used to be monopolised by entrants from the home countries of the UK.

The 1997 annual meeting was held at Scarborough. This was the end of my presidency and I handed over the reins to Joe Preston, who had been a tremendous vice president for me.

The highlight of that meeting for me was a gift from the American Farriers Association President, Lim Couch, whom I had met on a few occasions. His big claim to fame, other than being national President, was that he had also shod horses for Elvis Presley.

The gift was two horseshoes, beautifully framed. They had been made for Elvis' walking horse, Ebony's Secret Threat, a very special yearling that had been a champion. The permission to donate the shoes to me had to be requested from Graceland. Although Elvis had died by this time, the horse was still going strong and lived into its thirties. That was a very special gift to end my presidency.

So we drove home, relieved to have finished our term as 'Mr President and his Lady', but satisfied that we had achieved most of what we had set out to do.

However, having seen the glitz and glamour, it was back now back down to earth for me with my old working clothes on Monday!

Being presented with Elvis Presley's
horseshoes by American Farriers
Association President, Lim Couch.

Chapter 9

Calgary Before and After

WORLD championships in most sports and pursuits are held in various parts of the world. Mostly they move around from country to country, although others stay put. With its world famous stampede and with plenty of horse ranches in the surrounding countryside, Calgary was an obvious permanent site for a world championship farrier competition.

The first one was held in 1979 but initially it did not get much publicity in Britain. The competition first came to my attention a year or two later when a friend in Vancouver whom I had met at another international event suggested that I should come over and take part.

It happened that Mairi and I were due to celebrate our silver wedding in 1982 and we thought we could combine a holiday in Canada with competing at Calgary. Along with friends – a local joiner and his wife – we booked our flights and I submitted my entry to the competition.

Some three months ahead of the event, a letter from the organisers arrived. It contained the schedule of the type of shoes I would be required to make. They were mostly a different style from what I was used to, so the first exercise for me was to work out the sizes and methods of making them. I also noted that the time limits for most classes were much tighter than I was used to in this country, so a good and efficient working system was going to be very important. With a fair bit of practice under my belt by the time we left for Calgary I had most of the shoes mastered.

The four of us planned our holiday around Calgary, the stampede and the competition, and also scheduled a series of visits to friends and relations whom we had not seen for years and sometimes decades.

We aimed to spend the first week with Mairi's relatives in Victoria, Vancouver Island, and then go to a small town some fifty miles out of Calgary, before heading into the city and the competition.

In those days, Prestwick Airport in Ayrshire was the main international base for flights to North America. The airline we used was Wardair, which a few years later was taken over by Canadian Airlines. We flew out on a Boeing 747. This was our first experience of flying in such a massive aircraft and we all wondered how on earth it would get off the ground.

The plane touched down at Calgary on the way out in order to let some passengers off, but we continued on to Vancouver where Mairi's cousin had arranged to pick us up. Identifying her was no problem as she was the double of Mairi, proving the family genes were strong.

After a week seeing the sights, including a guided tour through the parliament buildings, where the most spectacular things we saw were the beautiful brass gates, it was time to move on.

Before we did, though, we met Bob Marshall who was staying nearby. It was he who had originally suggested that I should come to Calgary to compete. I also met another farrier, Dave Ducket, with whom I was to be working in the two-man team competition at Calgary. Never one to give up an opportunity to practise, especially as it was important to find out if there were any practical differences in working as a farrier in Canada, I soon persuaded him to get his smiddy fire lit and we had a go.

This was helpful in that I found out that their fires were different from ours. We have side-draught fires while the Canadian ones were up draught, the difference being that the air from the fan comes in from the side with ours, while theirs comes up from the bottom. The actual fire, which uses either coal or coke, reacts differently, so trying it out before the competition was a good idea.

Soon, with the days ticking by and the competition moving closer, we were heading into Calgary by train. I thought this would be a good way to see the countryside but it turned out to be a disappointment as all through the train journey, the weather was very misty. Added to that was the fact that half the travel was done during the night. All I remember was a long, long train with many carriages and the fact that we seemed to be amongst trees most of the time. I was glad when we arrived in Calgary after twenty-three hours, although just before we arrived in the station, the train had to be thoroughly washed and sprayed, which, again, seemed to take for ever.

The next day we went to the stampede ground to register and have a look around. We were going to be working in a huge marquee covered in rubber sheets that were coloured red and white. For obvious reasons it was known as the 'big top', although since my first year there it changed its name depending on which commercial company was the main sponsor.

Back in 1982, we had to supply our own anvil and fire and I don't think that any airline would have been too happy to allow me to bring my equipment over from Scotland, so my friend from British Columbia organised and brought two fires and anvils over in his truck. It was an eighteen-hour drive, but that just seemed to be a normal length of journey to him.

First thing the next morning we were down early for the 'eagle eye' competition. In this class, the competitor is allowed to look at a horse's foot for ten seconds then gets fifteen minutes to make a shoe to fit. This shoe is judged on size, only unfortunately my shoe was too big and was eliminated; a bad start to the competition. Mairi was in the stand beside the judges and could not believe it when my effort was chucked into the scrap heap. No prizes for that one, I thought ruefully.

The next competition was the 'Mustad Championship Forging Class', where competitors had to make three shoes: one aluminium and two steel shoes. This was more to my liking. I was really working well but was going too quickly, not realising that Calgary was four thousand five hundred feet above sea level and consequently the oxygen in the air was thinner. Suddenly my right arm completely seized up. I could not bend it at all. Thankfully I was so far ahead of my time schedule that I was able to stop for about five minutes and put my arm into a pail of cold water and also take some salt. I then started again and, thankfully, still finished on time. I was happy with my shoes and at the prize giving I was awarded first prize, as well as five hundred dollars and a bronze belt buckle for being the forging champion.

Being presented with the Forge Belt Buckle in
1982 by the sponsors – the Mustad family.

I should say it was called the Mustad championship after the sponsoring company, who are the biggest makers of horseshoe nails in the world. Curiously, the family firm, which was originally based in Switzerland, started making horseshoe nails in the same decade as my six times grandfather started as a blacksmith in Kilmany. Anglers may also recognise the Mustad name as, after a family fall-out, one brother went off and made fishing hooks and was so successful that these hooks are famed throughout the world. Over my competitive horseshoeing career, most of the events were either sponsored by Mustad or by Capwell, an American-based horseshoe nail-making company that Mustad bought over in 1985.

Day two of the competition was the live shoeing, which entailed making shoes for a horse and then shoeing it. The horse I drew in the ballot seemed quiet when I started, but apparently it had never been shod with hot shoes before and whenever I touched the foot and the smoke rose, the horse went crazy. Bill was holding the horse but did not have the experience to calm it down so another farrier stepped in and managed to contain it until I was finished. Despite all the trouble, I still took second place against strong opposition.

The last class was the two-man event. In this I was working with Dave Ducket. He was one point ahead of me going into the class, and every point I got he would get the same, so I knew I had no chance to win the championship. Bob Marshall was working with his dad. They came first and we were second. I finished up reserve world champion, which was not bad for my first visit. But as has been reported, it just whetted my appetite and I returned better prepared, more aware of the probable problems and very much focused on winning, all of which helped in my winning the world championship title.

After being World Champion the following year, in 1985, another pleasant surprise awaited me when I was asked to come back in 1986 to be one of the judges. This was a great honour as I was the first Scotsman to be invited to do so. When the competition schedule came out, I realised I was going to be very busy before I went to Calgary as the judges had to make all the specimen shoes for the competition. My co-judge was Gordon Height from America, whom I had never met. There were eleven shoes to be made and each shoe had to be of a very high standard as no doubt all the competitors would be very critical and look for any fault. I started making the sample shoes in March, and by the time we were preparing to leave for Calgary at the beginning of July, all were ready and I was very pleased with them.

Our flight went well and when we arrived the airport was buzzing with Canadians dressed in their jeans and Stetson hats, all in honour of the stampede. We were to meet a committee member who would

A big haul of rosettes, complete with the World
Championship trophy and one of the winning shoes.

take us to the hotel, and because I was judging, he had to be on call
whenever I wanted.

The first night we had a judges' meeting, initially with the show
committee to go over all the shoes. Gordon, my co-judge, had not
competed for a long time and he liked my shoes better than his own.
Most of mine went forward to the competitors' meeting, which was
perhaps a trifle embarrassing. However, I think it worked out all right
as judging is easier when competitors know exactly what they are
doing.

I was up very early next morning to be collected and taken to
the stampede ground. Judging is a totally different experience from
competing. We had about seventy competitors from all over the
world, and as some of them could not speak English, they had to rely
on an interpreter. We soon found it was often easier to communicate
with hand signals.

As soon as the shoes were made they were passed to us and very quickly shoes were coming at us from all sides. We had to work smartly to award them points and place them in order. Judging has changed over the years but that first year I was involved, we only kept the top six shoes on the table. The top six from the first heat were kept, then the top six from the second round were compared with the first round. Six were discarded, until the last round was finished, then the top six were placed in order. We worked together so that disagreement could be easily overcome.

This was not the case when we came to the live shoeing, as we judged separately and were on completely different wavelengths. We overcame this by adding the points together and dividing them by two, as we were never going to agree with each other: I thought that I was right and he thought he was right. Fortunately our different views did not affect the outcome of the competition.

It was good to see other people's point of view and even if I say so myself, I think we did a very good job. At least, most people were happy with our work. I certainly enjoyed the experience of judging at such a high standard and felt very proud to have been asked.

While I was judging, Mairi had a visit from her relatives from Vancouver and California and she invited them to the hotel for a drink. My friends had also promised a bottle of cognac and said they would meet me in the hotel.

I arrived back to our hotel room to enjoy a drink of this superb brandy after a hard day judging, only to find about half an inch in the bottom of the bottle. I suppose the old saying 'nothing lost that a friend gets' could be true, but it took a little while for me to accept that wisdom.

In 1987, I was off to Calgary again. This time our son David came with me and, as well as competing in all the classes, we were in the two-man team together.

This was David's first time in Calgary but I was an old hand by this time and we stayed with our friend Florence. It was just like being at home. As usual, we went down to the hotel to register and I introduced David to many of the other competitors. Magna Delabeck was there from Norway and he and David hit it off and have remained friends ever since.

The competition started, and we picked up some rosettes and were going along well. Then the two-man team class came along. This was to be our main one, and was really the purpose of our visit. I am pleased to say that everything went along smoothly. We were finished on time and were content with the quality of our work, but it was quite nerve wracking waiting for the results.

Again they started at sixth place, then fifth and when it came down to second and our names still hadn't been read out, the excitement grew. Then with his voice rising all the time, the announcer shouted out, 'First place goes to David Wilson senior and David Wilson junior from Scotland.' That was one of my proudest moments and a lump came into my throat. As part of a father and son team winning the world championship two-man team event, I felt even more emotional going up for our rosettes than I did when winning the world championship in 1985. When I think about that moment, I can still hear the tremendous cheer from the spectators and our fellow competitors.

This win put me into the top ten with points to spare. After that, the rest was just a blur in my memory, as we had won the class that we had set out to win.

Over the years, I have competed seven times at Calgary and although I have never been champion again, I always managed to get into the top ten, the last time being in the year 2000 when I was sixty-three years old. Everyone thought that this was quite amazing as the competition covers a very strenuous four days. On my last competition in Calgary, I almost hoped that I would not make the top five, as I had no energy left.

As well as judging in 1986, I have gone on to judge the world championships another four times, the last time being in 2012. This is a record as no one has judged it more than twice before. This probably came about because I had a lot of input into the system early on when the competition was growing. Twenty twelve was the centenary of the Calgary stampede and it was an honour to be invited back to judge such a special event.

The format has changed over the years and in 2012 we judged behind curtains with the horses being brought to us. That year, I judged with Shane Carter from America, with whom I had previously judged. This new format had been introduced two or three years before but I felt it took away a lot of the atmosphere not to be working in front of the spectators. I think also the competitors lost some of their time and momentum when their horses were taken away, having to just wait until they were judged and brought back to them.

The first round of competitors did not realise how fast they would have to work and the second round caught up with the first round. At one point, we had seven horses standing waiting to be judged, and it was pretty hard going as Shane and I each lifted two hundred and eighty horses' feet the first day of the competition.

Calgary has been a very important part of my life and has become such a special place to me.

Chapter 10

Australian Travels

WHEN the telephone rang in the Wilson home about four o' clock one morning, Mairi and I both awoke with a start. The phone sounded just like an alarm bell. Something is wrong with the family, was our first thought, but no, it was an Australian voice that responded to my sleepy answer. Initially I wondered if some of my good blacksmith friends were winding me up, but the voice was sincere and it was inviting me over to judge and give horseshoeing clinics in five states in Australia.

The trip was planned to take five weeks. We would start off with the world draught horse shoeing competition in Brisbane and then move to Sydney followed by Melbourne and Adelaide. The trip would finish up at the national horse shoeing championships in Fremantle, Western Australia.

Even although Mairi and I had been sound asleep when the phone rang, I reckon it took all of ten seconds for us to decide to say yes. There was no more sleep that night. We came downstairs and made tea, got the map out and looked at all the places we would be going to. We considered it was an unbelievable honour to be asked to help the Australians to improve their horseshoeing industry.

Having been brought up in an era when Australia was seen as being far, far away, we hardly believed that someone on the other side of the world would phone us in a small village in Scotland with that invitation. We also talked about the original Wilson blacksmith in the early years of the nineteenth century only knowing Australia as a penal colony, if he knew about it at all.

The pride in being asked to judge, advise or speak to other blacksmiths in other parts of the world has never left me. Since that call, there have been other invitations from different countries to pass on my knowledge and skills. I never, ever take such requests for granted or am blasé about receiving them.

Mairi and I spent several early-morning hours talking about the trip, but having said yes we did not delay making our plans. We went into the travel agent the very same day to make the arrangements to fly to Sydney where we would pick up tickets for our internal flights.

As a young man brought up in the 1950s, I recall some of my school friends taking up the offer of a ten-pound one-way ticket to

Australia as that country tried to entice more people to come to live and work there. At that time, with a lengthy six-week sea journey, it was reckoned that unless something dramatic happened, we were saying goodbye for ever to those who took the ten-pound trip. Well, as we all know, the something 'dramatic' was air travel and many of those who made the one-way trip in the 1950s have now travelled back to the old country, some of them many times.

However, air travel to the other side of the world is still a long haul. We left Balmullo on Monday 27 April 1992 in the early afternoon and flew from Edinburgh to Heathrow where we embarked on a twelve-hour flight to Singapore. A three-hour stop there was supposed to provide a rest period, but there was no rest and we boarded the plane for the final leg of the journey to Sydney.

As we stepped out of the aeroplane it was like walking into an oven. It was so hot and the day was just starting as it was only just after six in the morning. Making it worse, my body was still convinced it was six thirty at night.

We were met by Billy Neville and his wife Heather, whom we had actually met before in Calgary, Canada. A number of years later, they arrived without notice at our home in Balmullo. They had refused our offer of hospitality as they said they were heading off to friends who lived in Dundee. We said our farewells and sat back in our chairs to

Attending to a laminitic horse with Keith Swan
on our first night in Australia.

Mairi and I relaxing after work with Keith Swan.

think of the chat we might have had if they had stayed. Our thoughts were interrupted by a car drawing up outside. They had come back to stay with us, as their friends were no longer living in Dundee. But that was all in the future, as they outlined our Australian itinerary in the searing heat of Sydney airport.

The first leg of our whirlwind trip around the continent saw us jump right back on a plane to travel to Brisbane. This was only a one-hour flight from Sydney and we were met there by Keith Swan, the Australian National President of the Australian Farriers Association. We stayed with Keith and his wife Camilla for the duration of our time in Queensland.

Our luggage was piled into their truck and our first stop was the local farrier-supply business so he could stock up on horseshoes and nails, and then on to see a lame horse that had laminitis. Eventually, we made it to their home where, despite having been on our feet for the best part of two days and both now exhausted, we found out that a cup of tea and a dram – or that might have been two of the latter – put new life into us.

Just to prove this was no holiday, I was out in the workshop the next morning at seven o'clock making specimen shoes for the forthcoming competition. Then it was down to the showground at Gatton where the competition was to be held the following day. The visit was necessary so I could check that everything was in order.

On the drive over there, I saw how important agriculture was to the economy of this small town, with its many machinery dealers and feed mills lining the main thoroughfares. My musings on the surrounding countryside were rudely interrupted with the request that I give a television interview while I was at the showground. I had to adjust to the marked Australian twang of the interviewer and he had to cope with my Fife accent, but other than that the interview went well.

The following day was the start of the world draught horse shoeing competition. There were teams from most of the states in Australia as well as one from New Zealand.

I had never seen a three-man horseshoeing team at work before. It was a completely new format to me, as we do not have this type of thing in Britain. One man trimmed the feet while the other two made the shoes. In the first place, the shoemakers looked at the feet before they were trimmed. The shoemakers then cut off the steel for the shoes. If the man who was trimming the feet had pared back the hooves too heavily, the shoemakers could end up with a totally different shape of shoe for the trimmed hoof.

It was difficult for me to judge as some of the shoes just would not fit and I could not allow them to be nailed on. Some of the competitors had not shod many draught horses before but I eventually came up with a result that saw the team from New Zealand acclaimed as winners, with the local Queensland team second.

The next day there were forty people at the clinic in Keith's workshop where I showed them how to overcome some of the

An eight-horse team pulling a road scraper as
part of a demonstration at Gatton.

problems they had encountered in the competition. The temperature in the workshop was almost too hot to work in but it was a dry heat. At one point, a cloud went over the sun, the humidity just shot up and the sweat poured from me. I had to keep drinking water to stop my body from dehydrating.

With all the judging and demonstrating going on, I hardly had time to take in much of the local life. I do know that both Mairi and I have always enjoyed watching the long slow sunsets back home, but here in Gatton it was just as if someone had switched off the light at the end of the day.

One minute we were sitting with our hosts in the evening light and the next it was pitch black. This change from day to night seemed to be the trigger for the local cricket population, as the air was soon filled with the sound of thousands of the little insects.

There was a different sound in the morning when the chatter of kookaburras wakened us as soon as the sun came up. This was just as well as we had an early start to our journey to New South Wales.

Again we met up with the Nevilles, who would be our hosts for the next ten days. Thankfully we had some leisure time and we saw the sights in Sydney including the iconic Sydney Harbour Bridge and the famous Opera House. I now understood why the locals sometimes referred to the building as 'the flying nuns', with its unique shape of roof.

A four-hour car drive took us to Muswellbrook, the Nevilles' home, which was out in the bush. But just as we were thinking how far from home we were, we called in at Colo, a little village the size of Balmullo that lies at the entrance to the main recreational area in New South Wales. There we met Dorothy Coutts, who runs a caravan park. Her folks live in the village of Strathkinnes, only a couple of miles from our home in Balmullo. After enjoying coffee and being given a bag of lemons from her trees, we continued our drive.

When we checked our itinerary before leaving Scotland, we had been intrigued to find the Muswellbrook area described as famous for its coal mines and its horse breeding. If these seemed two totally different spheres of life, there was comfort in finding out that it was also famous for producing Hunter Valley wine.

The Nevilles' house was completely made of wood and it lay in an area of breathtaking scenery and utter tranquillity, thus making it all very attractive and very different from our stone-built home back in Scotland.

For the first three days with the Nevilles, I went out shoeing horses with Bill and his boys from early morning – and I mean early, as the work started about 5.30 am – and we kept going until late at night.

Their business was mainly shoeing racehorses: foals, brood mares and the stallions.

With a few days free before and after the competition I was able to do some sightseeing. As a result, I can confirm that some of the stud farms up in the Hunter Valley were superb.

With one hundred-plus years in existence, Widden Stud, which we visited and which is owned by the Thompson family, has a reputation for breeding some of the top sires in the country. It is located in a beautiful natural valley with mountains all around.

A century ago, the Bell Trees Station covered a quarter of a million acres. It had been massive. Especially when I compared it with my home county of Fife which is just over one-third of a million acres. Bell Trees had shrunk by the time Mairi and I visited it, but it had retained its horse-breeding programme and, to make us feel more at home, its herd of Aberdeen Angus cattle. We were shown through the original homestead, which was like something from the deep south of the United States of America. Bell Trees has been owned by the White family since 1806. The Mrs White who owned it when we visited was the sister of Anthony Armstrong-Jones, who married Princess Margaret, the sister of Queen Elizabeth.

We also visited the Segenhoe Stud, where we became aware of the vast amounts of money that go into horse breeding. This very large stud is now owned by Sydney-based businessmen and the horses are right at the top end of the pedigree world.

Back to work, however, I had to make specimen shoes before the competition to take place in Scone, which has the nickname of 'horse capital of Australia'. Both Mairi and I had problems pronouncing the name, as we both know the town of Scone in Scotland. It is pronounced 'skoon' while this Australian version insisted on being pronounced 'skon', as per the tea bread we eat back home.

The competition was carried out over two days and it went well. There were actually three different competitions: the first was for novices, the next was for anyone who had never won a first prize and the premier one was the open class.

After prize giving, Mairi and I were presented with two champagne glasses from the New South Wales branch of the Australian Farriers Association.

Before we knew it, we were off on the next stage of our trip, this time to Melbourne in the State of Victoria. The flight only took about one hour but it took us to colder and wetter weather more reminiscent of what we have back home. We were a bit apprehensive arriving at the airport as no one had told us much about our next host apart from the fact that the person's name was Robyn. Leaving the arrivals hall at the

Scone is the horse capital of Australia and the
local park has a statue of a mare and foal.

airport, we ran into the usual melee of people holding up name cards. Among them there was a girl holding a placard with the name Wilson and a horseshoe drawn alongside. It was quite eye catching. Wrongly we assumed her husband was the farrier but were soon put right when Robyn said she was.

Robyn and her husband had built their own house, but it is more accurate to state that it was an ongoing project. On their small farm they kept four horses, a Shetland pony, forty sheep, some cows, too many cats and the family dog.

The next day I was due to do a clinic at Ballarat, which meant an early start. It was held in Sovereign Hill, a heritage park that is still used like a working gold-mining village, with old shops and horse-drawn carriages. There was also an old blacksmith shop with a man working at the fire. Just as a moth is attracted to the light, so are blacksmiths drawn to a forge. I spoke to him and he asked how I had come from Scotland. 'I flew, of course,' I said. He looked at me and said, 'Flew?' He was in period dress and it took me a minute to realise he was having me on. He wanted to stay in character and during the gold rush days in Ballarat there had been no aeroplanes.

The clinic was held next day and it was the first to remind me of home as the weather was wet and cold. Tarpaulins had to be strung across trees over the anvils and fires to keep us dry while we worked but there was a good turnout for the clinic, even in the rain.

We spent that night with Paul Smith, a local farrier who took us to his parents' home. They had a small farm with Welsh show ponies and had been at the top of their field at one time with a supreme championship won at the prestigious Melbourne Show. Thankfully I knew a fair bit about Welsh Ponies, as Jock McKenzie had a lifetime's interest in them and would, with the slightest encouragement, talk at length about them.

After a day shoeing with Paul, we were on the move again, this time to Adelaide. Once more this was going to be a two-day clinic.

We were met at the airport by the President of the Australian Farriers Association, Ian Johnston, with whom we were to be staying for the duration of our time in the city. Again the clinics went well, with everyone keen to learn, and I actually saw the improvement by the second day.

The last lap of our journey was to Fremantle in Western Australia and by this time we were pretty fed up living out of suitcases. The national championships were held in the Fremantle Jail, which was no longer used for its original purpose. It was a good venue as it had very good workshops that were ideal for running a competition of this size.

The draught horse shoeing competition in Adelaide.

This visit to Western Australia was the main highlight for Mairi as we were going to be staying with her relatives. She had an aunt and two cousins in Perth and had not seen them for quite a number of years. Some thirty years previously, she had been a bridesmaid to one of the cousins and we stayed with her and her husband. There was a lot of family and local gossip they had to catch up on. The talking carried on well into the night and, in fact, continued the next day. Our hosts were desperate to show us the local countryside and it was good to have some time away from farriers and horses for a few days.

Soon it was time for the national championships, with the usual meeting for judges and competitors prior to the event in order to go over the shoes for all the classes. Again the competition was in three different levels: open, intermediate and novice.

The novices just made simple shoes, as a first- and second-year apprentice would do in Britain. The intermediate class would make more difficult shoes and also fitted and nailed shoes on the horses. The open competition was mainly concerned with the making of therapeutic shoes for horses with faults in their feet, as well as handmade shoes fitted to the horses.

Again we had a three-man draught horse class, but this time there was an improvement from five weeks previously. There were competitors from every state and strong rivalry between the entrants. It was such a pleasure to judge and give clinics to so many people who were keen to learn and improve their skills.

The only problem during the competition came when two horses had to be sedated. The vet must have mixed up the doses he gave them as they both ended up nearly falling over.

I may have made the decisions during the competition but it was Mairi who handed out all the cups and prize tickets. I was presented with a lovely framed picture of myself taken in Keith's workshop five weeks earlier. We were also given a book about Australia from the AFA to remind us of our trip.

The evening finished about midnight and we said our goodbyes to so many friendly and good people, thinking that we would probably not see many of them again. We did not know at that time we would be back five years later.

And just to prove how small the world is these days, as we booked in for our long flight home, the girl at the check-in desk asked which part of Scotland we came from. After we told her, she said her father was the gamekeeper at Ayton Hill, which is less than one mile from where I worked with Jock McKenzie. In fact, I used to go to her father's shoots. She made sure we had good seats for our journey home.

Chapter 11

America

WHEN people tell me they have visited the United States I often ask which of the fifty States they have actually been to as it is such a vast country. It is like saying I have been to Europe without saying whether that is to Finland or Greece.

Over a twenty-year period from the mid 1980s, Mairi and I flew over the Atlantic seven times to visit various parts of the USA. Each visit had a different focus, but not surprisingly, they all related in one way or another to shoeing horses.

As a result, I can say I have been to most of the main parts of the States where horses are still an important part of life, whether that is on the racecourses in Kentucky or in the vast Mid West prairie lands.

The state of Kentucky is famous across the world for its racehorses and for making bourbon. It was for the former reason that Jock McKenzie and I and our wives headed there in 1988, where the American Farriers Association was holding its annual convention and its national competition.

Kentucky is nicknamed the Blue Grass State but as we headed to Lexington from our hosts, Buddie and Louise, through the Blue Ridge Mountains and the tunnels that now help the traveller cross the Appalachians, the grass was still brown from the winter frosts. Apparently we would have to come back later in the spring or summer to see the lush grass so called because of the type of soil that produces it. Seemingly, when the grass is blowing in the wind, it has a bluish tinge, but it was too early in the year for this and we pressed on as we had work to do.

There was an 'American saddle-bred shoe' on the national competition schedule. I was really not familiar with this, so I was given some advice from Danny Ward, a farrier friend, on how to make the shoe and the important points the judges would be looking for. He told me the saddle-bred horse was used in cotton plantations for the charge hand to ride around while keeping an eye on the workers. I seem to recall these charge hands often carried a horse whip that they did not limit to keeping the horse under control – but that is another matter. These horses had a very high knee action which was achieved by leaving a very long foot or, in some cases, fitting leather pads between the shoe and the foot. The shoe has a long clip forge

Jock McKenzie and I practising before
we head off to the States.

welded to the front. The nail holes were also near the inside edge of the shoe to make it easier to drive the nails in. While we were staying at Danny's farrier school in Martinsville, Virginia prior to the competition, Jock and I practised making this particular shoe.

Soon it was time to head off to the convention and the competition. I checked that all the tools we would need were properly set out, ready for action. We all managed to fit into Danny's massive truck along with the tools and luggage. From Martinsville to Kentucky is about four hundred and fifty miles but in American terms our journey was not considered to be lengthy.

Arriving in Lexington where the event was to take place, we set out to look for the Kentucky Horse Park in which the competition would be held. The Horse Park and the surrounding area were just as I imagined them to be with their white picket fences and a background of rolling hills. Surrounding the park were the privately owned racing stables, all of which had access to the racecourse for training. It was easy to see there was a lot of money in the area, judging by the big beautiful houses and well-maintained horse paddocks.

The hotel we were staying in was hosting both the main convention and acting as headquarters for the competition. After registration, we met many of the other competitors from all over the world; some of them I had met before at international competitions, but there were also some new faces from Japan and Europe.

After lunch Danny took us to an educational meeting where the future of farriery in America was discussed. It was very interesting to hear from farriers all over the country as they aired their different views. This was when I realised just how vast and how different the priorities and the concerns of the fifty States of America could be.

The next morning saw the start of the competition. It was in a totally different format to what either Jock or I was used to as all the competitors started at the same time. All the local farriers had brought their own rigs, complete with fires and anvils. Many were really travelling workshops. This left the competitors who had flown in to pre-book theirs and hope they could adjust to a strange forge.

I was allocated a big workshop van with the fire inside and the anvil on the ground outside, which meant I had to go up three or four steps from the fire to the anvil. It did not seem an issue at first, but after dashing between forge and anvil a few times I began to curse those steps.

However, before the competition began I had time to look around the arena. For all the world it reminded me of those cowboy films where the wagons were put in a circle to prevent the Indians attacking at night. There were sixty to seventy workshop trucks all with smoke belching out from the forge chimneys and all spaced out round the circumference of the big arena.

The first class was a shoemaking competition and we had to make four shoes. I worked out a format on how I would do this. I started with the two shoes that were the heaviest and got them finished, then the third one, with the intention of leaving the very light one until last, but I got carried away with myself and against my better judgment I started to make the fourth one as well. The controls on the fire were different, as the switch went clockwise to turn the fire off, and of course, I turned it the wrong way. When I went back up the four steps from the anvil to the fire, the shoe was burnt to a frazzle.

The spare steel was at the other end of the arena, about one hundred yards away. With the competition clock ticking, I had to run all the way there and back. Actually I walked the last thirty yards otherwise

I might well have suffered a heart attack. The effort was worth it as I managed to make the final shoe. I finished up with two really good shoes, one reasonable shoe and the fourth complete but not very good. When the shoes were judged and the points added up, I finished fifth. A result with which I was more than happy considering the circumstances.

The next competition was a pair of heart bar shoes. With this, the bar across the shoe gives support to the foot. By now everything was going to plan and I finished up with a fourth prize. The results were getting better. The question was, could I keep improving? Next came the draught horse two-man team competition with the competitors paired up. Jock and I were lucky to get a forge right beside the anvil. I reckon I had done quite enough running up and down the steps into the truck. The actual competition was over in a flash and we finished easily within the time, and without being complacent we were pleased with the work.

The last class was the horse shoeing. We had to make and fit a shoe to a horse's foot and also to make a specimen shoe. It was a caulk and wedge shoe that they wanted. This was made out of one-inch by a half-inch metal bar with a caulking and wedge heels. Again without being smug, I was pretty happy with the finished article, but it would be later that night at the banquet when I would find out if my good feeling was justified, when the judges announced their verdict and the prizes were handed out.

At the banquet we were all dressed up in our best bib and tucker, Mairi in a ballgown and me in my Wilson tartan kilt. The dining area was massive and sat more than a thousand people, but then this was America where everything had to be bigger than back home. The people at our table were not farriers and were strangers to us so there was not a lot of conversation going on during the meal.

When the results for each class were read out and I went up for my fifth prize in the forging class and then fourth in the heart bar shoes, my dining companions began to take notice. This was followed by the announcement of the results of the two-man team and Jock and I were first. By this time, our neighbours were obviously impressed and started to ask questions about the two Scots competitors sitting at their table. The last class was the shoeing class and I was thrilled to win and to be awarded the North American Challenge Cup. Everyone came round to our table to congratulate Jock and I. By now our fellow diners were our best friends and a super time was had by all.

This was the first time the North American Challenge Cup had been awarded out of the country, and it was coming home with me to Balmullo.

Jock McKenzie and I with our awards in Lexington.

It was back to business the next day, when Jock and I were taken to a vets' practice which dealt mainly with laminitic and foot ailments. It was very interesting to see the different techniques for dealing with those problems, compared with what we practised in the UK.

After our visit to the vets' surgery, the manager of the world-famous Lanes End stud farm drove us to see the two-and-a-half-thousand-acre farm that is owned by the Farish family. Just to prove how small connections can sometimes lead to doors unexpectedly opening, this visit came about purely because the manager and Jock had a mutual friend who bred Welsh Ponies.

The stud farm was amazingly grand. When we approached the gate house, the manager signalled to the person on security and the big bollards in our path just disappeared into the ground. The first barn we came to was full of yearlings that would be for sale in the coming months. The next barn was for yearlings that were being kept and would go into training the following year.

About half a mile further along, we came to where the brood mares were housed. Each barn had its own paddock where the horses could run about freely during the day. The mares' boxes were big and had plenty of room for the foals. We saw one foal with his mum and were told he was valued at a million dollars. He was only seven days old! This was proof to me that we were being shown a top-market stud. Some of the mares were by famous sires such as Secretariat and Northern Dancer, both Kentucky Derby winners. Other mares were sired by Nijinsky who won the Epsom Derby and then went on to be one of the top sires in the world.

For animal disease reasons, any mare that came from another area was kept in a separate barn about a mile away. We were told the only owner who was allowed to have mares in the main stables was Her Majesty, Queen Elizabeth.

This was the most impressive stable and yard I have ever seen and I would love to have been employed as a farrier, but you can't have everything. I have Scotland and now I have many good friends in the state of Kentucky.

Two years later Mairi and I were back across the Atlantic. This time further west to Lubbock in the Lone Star State of Texas but we did not head there right away as we stayed in Kansas with our friends Ed and Michelle Zook. I had first met Ed several years before when he came over to Scotland on the student exchange scheme that was operating at that time and stayed with us in Balmullo.

The trip from the Zooks' home in Kansas down to Texas took us through some real cowboy country. It was a thirteen-hour drive through very flat country, passing places we had only heard of in Country and Western songs, towns like Oklahoma and Amarillo.

We arrived in Lubbock, which was bathed in the most amazing sunset that lit up the whole sky, as if the sky was on fire, but after the lengthy drive our own lights went out pretty quickly.

The competition was the next day and it went well. I won a few rosettes, but nothing to get excited about. It was a worthwhile exercise and I learned a lot.

Five years later I was invited back to Lubbock to judge the Texas Professional Farriers Association Competition and also to do a clinic. The competition I was to judge came only days after the UK Farrier International weekend at Stoneleigh, and being President of the Association that year, I was very much involved in organising that event. We arrived back home from our competition in England on the Tuesday and were away down to Dumfries on Friday to judge the Edward Martin competition the next day. Edward Martin and I had competed on many occasions and, as we shall discover, he was also a modernday pioneer in going over to America to take part in and judge competitions there.

We dashed back from Dumfries on Sunday and the following

Up, up and away. Our helicopter trip in Texas.

morning we were in Edinburgh airport with passports in hand as we headed off to Lubbock in Texas. There we were met by Mark Terry, a farrier who had also been on the student exchange scheme and who had also stayed with us in Balmullo. He took us to his home where we met his lovely wife, and where we spent a few days before the competition began. Mark drove us around, and one of the highlights was a helicopter flight with one of his clients over his ranch, which stretched for miles. We saw herds of deer, various types of antelope and mountain goats, all just running wild. We were up for thirty minutes and only saw a small part of his property. This was a wonderful experience. And to prove we were in Texas where everything is supposed to be bigger and better than anywhere else in the world, we had a barbeque with massive T-bone steaks – very, very tasty.

Our leisure time was soon over and the first task I had was to demonstrate shoeing a Clydesdale. This was no problem for me even if there was a television camera simultaneously interviewing me and recording the action as I worked. I have to mention the temperature was over a hundred degrees Fahrenheit, so I was drinking pints of Gatorade and also sweating buckets.

While I was hard at work, Mairi was able to walk around the showground, and discovered the Civic Centre where the Cowboy Symposium was held, as well as Country and Western music. She had a most enjoyable day, even though I was wondering where she had disappeared to – in fact, I had to go looking for her. The day finished with a big banquet and prizegiving as well as a dance, which suited Mairi and me admirably as we love dancing. The chairman's wife had composed and recited a poem about a lady farrier, which was probably a bit risqué but was very funny. Her husband thought it was dreadful that she had read her composition in David Wilson's presence, but little did he know that I had already asked her for a copy which sadly I was unable to find on my return home. Was it confiscated at Customs as unsuitable material to enter the UK? I do not know.

The following day saw us off to College Station, Austin where we were met by our hosts Don and Cathy Sustaire. If I had thought Lubbock was warm, it was nothing compared to our latest stop, with the humidity hitting ninety-five percent and the temperature over the hundred-degree Fahrenheit mark. Just to walk from the house to the workshop, which was about thirty yards, saw me burst out in sweat. All the time I was working at the forge, they had a big fan with a drip feed of water blowing a fine mist over me to keep me cool. One of the farrier's sons, who was going to work with his dad in the competition, was told to sit down right in front of me and really pay attention. Unfortunately, he fell asleep so I put water on the anvil and brought a pure-white horseshoe out of the fire, put it on the water and gave it a good chap with my hammer. The noise this made was like a shotgun going off. He jumped straight up about six feet out of the chair and I can assure you he didn't fall sleep again!

As a diversion that evening after the clinic, I was invited to go out hog hunting. There were a few men and a pack of hounds on the hunt. It was not really my idea of enjoyment but I thought it might be a good experience. The grass we were walking through was long and it reached my waist. The walking was not made easier by it being really warm and humid. To make my life easier, I was like a good collie dog and kept right behind the man in front. That was also just in case there was a snake in our path. At one point our intrepid hunting gang ventured into a thicket of scrub and we had to retrace our steps as there was no way through. When the darkness came down they gave me a torch to let me see where all the spiders were. It was certainly not a place for people who do not like those insects as they had bodies about the size of a fifty-pence piece and their cobwebs hung from the branches like washing on a line. It was definitely not my cup of tea. It was after midnight before they called

106

a halt to the hunting, I was glad when we got back to the vans and I never saw a hog yet.

On the move again but still in Texas, we travelled to Houston, where we stayed with the President of the Texas Farriers Association and his wife. Forrest is a retired headmaster who was interested in farriery and now, in retirement, he does it full time while his wife, Julia, still teaches.

During this visit, I was invited to a vets' practice with the farrier and his friend, a big American with a Stetson and neck tie. When we were introduced to the secretary, Forrest said, 'Meet my friend from Scotland.' Her reply surprised me as she said, 'Which one?'

A year later, we were off on our travels again and this time our main destination was Kansas where the American Farriers Convention was being held. I was now President of the British Association and was treated as a VIP, which meant, among other perks, being given an executive suite in the hotel, which was rather nice.

I was still competing but I must have realised I was getting old because my aim this time was to get into the top twenty to qualify for the live shoeing on the final day. This I achieved and finished up sixth overall.

1997 marked my sixtieth birthday and we were again invited across the Atlantic, this time to Albuquerque in New Mexico. It was cold and wet when we left Edinburgh and optimistically we thought we would

Which one is the Texan?

An outdoor clinic in Texas under the sun.

be flying into much warmer weather in the States. What a shock it was when we arrived in Albuquerque. We thought it would be warm but it was below freezing and we had to open our cases and put on extra clothes before leaving the airport. Again I made the top twenty to qualify for the final and I came tenth overall. Everyone thought my performance was amazing apart from myself. I had never ever entered a competition to be thrilled with tenth place, but I suppose that is old age for you.

A year later and we were headed out to California, this time to judge the North American Classic competition. It was held in a place called Placerville, near Sacramento. We were met at the airport by Sharon Capps, whose husband is a farrier, and we were staying with them until the competition started.

In complete contrast with previous sun-filled steamy hot visits to the States, the rain just poured down when we arrived and it poured for two days. There was water everywhere. Farmers were concerned about their vineyards getting mildew and even the rice fields were flooded.

The competition ran well and everyone seemed to be quite satisfied with the results. I was given a standing ovation after I made my speech, so I reckon they were pleased with the judging and the teaching.

I should have mentioned that this was a special visit as Mairi was celebrating her sixtieth birthday during our time in the States. On the night of the prizegiving, an auction was held, and not having had time to get a birthday present, I thought this sale would provide an answer. I noticed a handmade silver necklace with all the farrier's tools handcrafted on it. It was beautiful, but, as is the way of such sales, someone else thought so too, and the bidding kept going up. Mairi was trying to keep my hand down to stop bidding. However, the other bidder eventually gave up and I managed to acquire the necklace.

Now, having secured Mairi's present, we headed into Nevada, calling at Virginia City and the Bucket of Blood saloon where we saw the famous selection of horseshoes. I did try the gaming machines but thankfully was given very limited time in which to lose money. From there we headed to Lake Tahoe to celebrate Mairi's birthday by the lake.

The silver horseshoes and the gaming machines
in the Bucket of Blood saloon.

The new millennium brought a most unexpected honour for me as I received a Farriers Legend Award from the *American Farriers Journal*. This meant a great deal to me as this is a most respected and well-read magazine throughout America. The citation also mentions that in 1995 I was inducted into the Kentucky Hall of Fame.

We went back to Kansas in 2001 but this time I was to be one of the judges, which proved to be quite a task. My two co-judges were Americans I have known for many years and we were all on the same wavelength, so although we were kept very busy, it was a pleasant atmosphere.

With no heats and all the competitors working at the same time, there was a flurry of shoes coming at us needing to be judged at the same time.

The first class was to make four shoes, two front and two hind, for a pleasure horse. These were to be just plain standard shoes. There were eighty competitors, so, in short order, we had to place one hundred and sixty pairs of shoes.

The next class was started as we were still deliberating the results of the first competition. This was the 'eagle eye' where, as previously explained, the competitor gets a ten-second look at a horse's foot then they have to make a shoe to fit in fifteen minutes. By the time we had about half of class one judged, another eighty shoes landed on the table before us. We worked until nearly midnight to clear the backlog and finish day one.

On day two at the live shoeing, we each judged one part. I judged the trim of the foot, checking the level and ensuring there was a nice symmetrical wall with no rough edges. Another judge checked the shoe and the fit. His responsibility included looking at the size and perimeter fit and that all the nail holes were in the right place on the shoe. This left the last judge to ensure the nailing and finish, with all the nails left in a straight line and all smooth and tidy.

I found it was a great experience and honour to be asked to judge the American Convention and a pleasure to work with two really good craftsmen and friends. I have done a lot of judging over the years, but nothing beats competing.

Our last trip to America came in 2008 when I was asked to judge the Edward Martin Classic in Reno, Nevada. As mentioned earlier, Edward and I had competed in Scotland and we had both crossed to the other side of the Atlantic to take on the American farriers in their own back yard. I had also judged his last competition in Closeburn, Dumfriesshire some years earlier. Now, following his death, a new competition in his honour was being held in Reno where, apart from the lady who was organising the competition, we also met some of

Mairi's relatives for the first time. It was surprising to me just how many people there had Scottish connections.

The event was high profile and before we were underway I was presented with letters from the Secretary of Agriculture, Washington DC, Edward T. Schafer. There was also one from the Governor of Nevada, Jim Gibbons, and the City Fathers did not miss out with their own letters of welcome. What made it more special for Mairi and me was that her cousin Chip MacLeod presented the citations.

The competition went well, with a lovely friendly atmosphere, and finished off with more letters being presented to me: one from the California Department of Food and Agriculture and one from the Secretary of State for California.

Over the years, spending time in the USA has been a great experience, and although I have given them the benefit of my years of experience in the farrier industry, I have had so much more in return.

Chapter 12

From the Other Side of the Fireplace

THE old saying that goes, 'behind every good man is a good woman' may apply in some cases, but throughout my career Mairi has stood by my side. Without Mairi's quietly given advice, I would not have had the success I have enjoyed and, equally importantly, I would not have enjoyed it as much as I have. When I was National President she had to reply to the Toast to the Ladies on two occasions. She decided to make her speeches in verse, and carried on writing poems for different occasions; some were composed while I was hammering out what I hoped were winning shoes or when I was chairing the many meetings.

Reflections on Life at
Balmullo Smiddy

Almost forty years ago
to Balmullo town we came,
to start a thriving business
and make ourselves a name.

Mairi giving her response in verse.

We arrived with three wee girls,
folks said that we were mad,
to give up home and wages
for that was all we had.

We started one December morn,
the frost was all around.
David started in the fire
fixing ploughs to work the ground.

Farmers soon saw the chimney smoking
and thought, What's happening there?
So it wasn't long until they came
with their machinery to repair.

Then the working Clydesdale
from the farm just down the road,
came to get his shoes on
to help him ease his load.

Ponies they were a plenty
and needed shoeing too,
the riding schools and stables
they all had work to do.

Then joy of joys we had a boy,
a cause for celebration.
Will he be a farrier too –
the seventh generation?

We employed some men to help with work –
the engineering grew.
They've been with us for many years,
perhaps I'll name a few.

First there's Robin Steven,
who's worked with us for years.
He's the one with the boiler suit
and cap around his ears.

He's such a reliable fellow,
never ever late,
you can hear his engine revving
at round the ten to eight.

Then we hear a motorbike
roaring along the straight –
that'll be Calum MacPherson,
nearly always late!

For excuses he's the master
of many an unlikely tale,
but a likeable chap,
a handsome lad,
and married now to Gail.

Then there's foreman Leslie Spence,
who married an Island dame.
She has the language of the Gael
and Leslie she did tame.

He does a lot of welding
and helps relieve the pressure

by drawing pictures,
doing pricing
and being quite a treasure.

The years have gone –
the family's grown
into these wiser adults,
and if you listen carefully
I'll relate their varied credits.

First of all there's Margaret,
an artist she is to trade,
she freelances for an English firm
and I think she gets well paid!

Then Ann does interior furnishings,
with the needle she's so dandy.
If your curtains need a nip and tuck
phone Ann, she's fine and handy!

Then if you're ill and feeling blue,
your symptoms getting worse,
you'll soon improve and brighten up
with Donna our district nurse.

Then David is the farrier.
He buys and sells the shoes.
If ever you need your horses shod
then he's the one for you.

They all have children of their own
and often arrive upon us –
we love them all so dearly,
to us they're such a bonus!

We reflect upon the forty years
of happy times and sad.
We think of friends no longer here
and the parents that we had.

We think about achievements,
and humbled by the thought,
no matter what we did ourselves

God's hand was the hand that wrought.

It's time to take life easier now
and watch the world go by.
To sit under a chestnut tree
and watch the pigeons fly.

Whatever it is that lies ahead,
or if it's mapped already,
we've really enjoyed the time we've had
and our life here at the smiddy.

This was the first speech Mairi had to give as the President's wife. It was made in Cardiff in 1995 as a reply to the Toast to the Ladies by Tom Burch, an English farrier. She had never ever made a speech before and thought it would be better done as a poem.

Cardiff Speech in 1995

The world today, it's fair to say,
is changing all the time,
that's why I thought I'd catch the flow
and make this speech in rhyme.

To Tom Burch, and the things you said,
you truly made us laugh,
a big thank you from the ladies,
I endorse on their behalf.

In moments of reflection,
when I look back upon my life,
I had no recollection,
I'd be a farriers wife!

High stepping at a village dance,
t'was there we chanced to meet,
I gave him an engaging glance
that swept him off his feet!

As time went by, we soon were wed,
our business was begun,
as well as shoes and gates, we made,
three daughters and a son!

When competition time comes round,
It's always plain to see,
before that perfect shoe is found
the friendly rivalry!

If you should roam the whole wide world,
no better will you meet,
than that faithful band of farriers
who tend the horses' feet.

The only grace our men may lack,
is incentive to retire,
and the main thing that would keep them back,
are those irons in the fire!

Now just before I end this screed,
a Welsh phrase I recall,
Diolch un vower e chee geed,
a big thank you to you all.

If you're ever in Balmullo,
near the county town of Fife,
you're assured a friendly welcome,
from the President and his wife.

The following poem was composed as Mairi sat with all the other
wives, girlfriends and partners during the many competitions the
menfolk took part in.

The Lament of the Farrier's Wife

Competitions, competitions, that's all I ever hear!
the dates come in, the shows begin,
they come round faster every year!

I look at all the schedules,
and see all the fancy shoes,
cock and wedges, concave, fullered
and even some that glues!

Perfection is the ultimate quest,
attained by very few,

they practise hard day in day out,
to make the perfect shoe!

They travel o'er the country,
in fact, throughout the world,
tending seminars and clinics
gaining knowledge all the while.

These farriers are a breed alone,
they're close and all collaborate,
can converse in any language
using hands to demonstrate!

As farriers' wives, we tend the shows,
the social gatherings too,
but we must think of a plan
to compete with the men,
while they're talking about horseshoes!

Reflections on a Year from the Wife of the President

We've just finished our term of presidency,
I sigh a sigh of relief.
The duties, the letters, the phone calls, the faxes,
were away beyond belief!

We've been up at the crack of dawn each day,
we've burned the midnight oil,
tending to many different tasks
and at daily work we toil.

I've packed so many suitcases,
whether we're driving or going by plane,
going back to our old daily routine,
somehow, life just won't be the same.

We've travelled the length and breadth of the country
(the airlines have really done well!),
to fly from Scotland to England,
their profits we really did swell!

We've travelled throughout the United States,
we've been to so many places,
we've met so many kindly folk,
I remember their friendly faces.

We spent some time in Aussie land,
saw koalas and kangaroos,
did various different clinics
and saw lots of Clydesdale shoes!

We've been wined and dined
by the elite of the world,
we've seen how the other half live,
but now I'll be happy to settle again,
some time to my family, I'll give.

And after another year accompanying David as President.

Twelve months ago in Cardiff, our presidency
    did begin,
how naïve I was to think it would be an easy
    thing,
our first event was the Mansion House, to London,
    we went by air,
the Lord Mayor was there to greet us
and Dr Garnham was in the chair.

The architecture was magnificent,
the décor a wonderful hue,
the dresses, the speeches, the food and the toasts,
it was indeed a memorable 'do'.

Next our Royal Highland Show,
Ingliston was the venue,
David was the chief steward
and I prepared the menu.

We travelled back and forth each day,
the traffic was horrendous,
but much to everyone's surprise,
the weather was tremendous!

Then in July, we packed our car
without any hesitation,
Stoneleigh and the Royal Show,
that was our destination.

Beautiful wrought-iron gates were made,
by the late Peter Walker,
and dedicated by William Waldegrave,
Ex-Minister of Agriculture.

Billy Crothers won the Royal Show,
with Dave Smith in close contention,
Gary Darlow won the Nationals,
They all deserve a mention.

They came from across the Atlantic,
the Pacific ocean too,
they crossed the English channel,
they came from Scotland too,
to take part in the International,
that was their intent,
to represent their country
in this prestigious event.

They came from North,
they came from South,
they came from East and West,
they made the shoes and shod the horse
to find out who was best.

Great excitement in the hall,
when the prize list was read out,
they raised their glasses filled with cheer
when Scotland won the count.

Then they all came up to Scotland
to Edward's competition,
to shoe these mighty Clydesdales,
that was their ambition.

We also had a ceilidh,
held in the village hall,
they played the Scottish music
and we really had a ball.

We appreciate all our sponsors,
for their participation and their grace,
without their generosity
our competitions would not take place.

Then we flew to Texas,
to judge a competition,
this was held in Lubbock,
David was the clinician.

I went to the Cowboy Symposium
and had a super time,
listening to country music
and cowboy poetry done in rhyme.

Then we flew to College Station,
to do a clinic there,
we stayed with well-known farriers,
Kathy and Don Sustaire.

The temperatures were in the hundreds,
the humidity almost as high,
I thought, is this moisture from my body
or is it falling from the sky?

The AFA Convention was next on the agenda,
we flew to Kansas City
in Missouri to attend it.

Mr President, sir, I thank you,
for your help throughout the year,
for your loving arms around me
on our travels far and near,

we look forward to the next twelve months,
with slight anticipation,
but rest assured, we'll do our best
for the Association.

Chapter 13

Looking Back

HAVING never before returned to my home patch as a world champion, I had no idea what to expect as I turned the corner into Balmullo. I did know that I would have to get back to my everyday work in my everyday work clothes. As the saying goes, 'When the boss is away, the mice will play.'

But getting back to work was not as easy as it might have been, because the phone never stopped ringing with congratulations from friends, family, farriers and blacksmiths.

No sooner was I home than I was interviewed for television news by the famous BBC news presenter Mary Marquis and the other interviewee was Sandy Lyle, the golfer, who had just won the British Open.

I was also interviewed on the radio by well-known Scottish broadcaster, Robbie Shepherd. I found this a most unusual experience as I was in the Dundee studio and he was in Aberdeen.

The phone rang constantly with reporters from local newspapers and national magazines wanting to know, among many other things, how I had managed to win a world championship despite coming from a small village in Fife.

It is often claimed that in a small community, such as Balmullo, everyone knows everything that goes on. That is definitely not true, as not long after I had returned home, Mairi suggested that we go out for a meal to celebrate. That sounded a great idea and it got even better when we passed the village pub and she suggested we went in for a drink first. I was amazed that she even suggested that. It was definitely a first.

As I stepped into the premises there was a loud cheer from the semi darkness. When all the lights were switched on I saw the room was packed with friends, neighbours, relatives, local businessmen, farmers and my employees; all were there because a couple of good friends, Jim and Ina Cameron, had organised a surprise 'David Wilson, this is your life'.

Once I got over the shock of it all, it turned out to be a brilliant night. I was presented with a chestnut tree with everyone remembering the poem that begins 'Under the spreading chestnut tree, the village blacksmith stands.' I planted it in the garden and it flourishes in the spring time with beautiful pink candles of flower buds. Visitors admire it and, so far, I have not admitted that the original tree did not survive, having been hit by a stray golf ball as I practised my swing. I only took up the sport in later life and local well-known golf professional, Jim Farmer, who was born and brought up in Balmullo, was heard to remark that I swung my golf clubs just as I used to swing hammers in the smiddy.

The chestnut tree that stands there now is a very healthy replacement, but any plan that I would sit under it and watch the world go by has yet to come to pass.

Another surprise at the 'This is Your Life' event came when the local joiner and Scottish dance band leader, Bobby Crowe, wrote a tune dedicated to me, a jig called 'David Wilson the Balmullo Blacksmith'.

When Bob was composing this, he was playing the accordion, recording the tune on tape, and to provide more atmosphere he persuaded his daughter, Alyson, to break three crystal glasses, which was the nearest he could get to reproducing the noise of hammering on the anvil.

Some time later, I received another honour from the village. A new small housing development had just been built and the community council named a street in it David Wilson Park. Normally, new roads are named after well-known people long after they have died but in my case they must have decided not to wait for that to happen.

Over the past two hundred years, there have been many working links between my family and the local landowners, the Kilmany family. The most recent one, which came out of the blue after my winning the world championship, was being awarded the British Empire Medal.

Although I did not know it at the time, Lord and Lady Kilmany were the instigators in putting my name forward for the honour, which states that the award is made in 'recognition of meritorious civil or military service'. I do not think my work welding pipes on the Leuchars air base would have earned me the honour, and this was confirmed with the wording 'for services to farriery in Scotland'.

As other award winners know, the big problem is keeping quiet after receiving the initial letter from Buckingham Palace and I was glad when the official announcement was made. Not long after, I had the medal pinned to my chest by Sir John Gilmour, then Lord Lieutenant of Fife.

My competitive success has also brought with it additional commitments, which have, in time, turned out to be good fun. I never did think I would become involved in public speaking but it all started with my brother looking for a speaker for his Probus Club. In a moment of weakness I agreed to talk on my fifty years as a farrier/

Planting the original chestnut tree after the world championships.

My very own Scottish dance music.

Former employees trying to say complimentary things about me at
'This Is Your Life'. From the left: Alan, Robin, Les and Alec.

Standing with a distant relation, also called David Wilson,
at the entrance to David Wilson Park.

David being presented with his British Empire Medal.

blacksmith. For weeks beforehand I worried about what I was going to say. I wrote down my speech and rehearsed it time after time. However, I was no sooner on my feet, with the Probus members in front of me, than I felt at ease, and that is how my public speaking career started. Mostly I am asked to speak to Rotary or Probus clubs but I now also address Church Guild and Women's Rural Institute meetings. The last always get their money's worth from a speaker, even if I do not charge, as I am asked to judge the competitions. Flower arrangements and best-baked cakes have all been subject to the judgment of David Wilson champion farrier, although I personally do not see my qualifications covering these subjects.

Now I seem to be on everyone's speaking list and have spoken to quite a number of groups. During question time at the end of my speech, I never fail to be surprised by how many people had grandfathers and great grandfathers who were blacksmiths. All of them show a great interest in some of the older and almost forgotten aspects of the profession.

Because of the long family tradition in the blacksmith trade and because both my son and grandson are now farriers, I can tell my audiences how vastly different the job is now compared with my day. The modern farrier has his mobile workshop, his van fitted out with gas forges, anvils and vices. There are no coal fires to light. He just switches on the gas furnace in the back of the van and heats the shoes.

Some farriers even have grinders and drilling machines that they just plug into the main electrical supply when they arrive at the stables. Nowadays, they are not visiting farms but livery yards and big stables. Some of the yards have over one hundred horses whose owners live in towns and keep their horses at livery. Changed days from when the work horses would arrive at the smiddy and be dealt with on a first-come first-served basis.

Another major difference today is that the farrier has machine-made shoes, which are manufactured to a very high standard in all different shapes and sizes suitable for small Shetland ponies to large hunters. These shoes need very little adjustment to fit the horse's foot. This allows the farriers to shoe more horses. In my day so much time was spent on actually making the shoes.

The modernday farrier also works on a pre-booking system and he or she can tell you where they will be in six weeks' time; again this is a vast improvement from my early days when farmers would turn up unexpectedly at the smiddy and expect immediate attention.

Although now well into my eighth decade, I still go into the old workshop to do small pieces of ironwork. 'Need to keep my hand in,' I say to Mairi as I escape some domestic chore. The work I do is mainly small railings for the front or back doors of houses. I am always surprised at how once someone in the street gets a safety railing at their front door, a neighbour sees it and thinks that's a good idea. They would like one too and before I know it I end up doing quite a few railings. I still have my coal fire and power hammer in the workshop

Off on a day's fishing on holiday in Skye.

Sorting the roof of the croft on Skye in
pre-Health and Safety Executive days.

and this makes life much easier. I also help fellow blacksmiths who do not have this facility.

So far, almost everything I have commented on has related to work, but Mairi and I have always had a lifeline away from this. Our house in Skye has over the years been invaluable as a perfect place to go and relax and get away from the pressure of business.

The house is situated on a hill and the croft extends down to the shoreline of Loch Bay, looking out towards the Atlantic Ocean and beyond to the Outer Hebrides. It is idyllic.

Mairi's great grandfather built the property in the early 1900s and it has been in Mairi's family for five generations. Mairi inherited the house in the late 1970s, along with twenty sheep.

Although I had plenty work to do on the Skye house and the croft, there always seemed to be time to stop for a 'strupag', which is Gaelic for a cup of tea. Also, in the relaxed attitude the locals have to life in Skye, I knew if I did not finish the job there was always tomorrow. One addition to the croft of which I am particularly proud, which also provides the ultimate in relaxation on a fine day, is the conservatory I built on the front of the house. This faces south and on good days the sun shines in all day long.

If the weather is fine, I will go out onto the sea loch in my boat, fishing for mackerel. Sometimes in all the hectic activity of relaxing in the boat, my mobile phone will ring. I answer it to find Mairi asking, 'Where are you? I can't see you,' or sometimes, 'Have you caught anything for tea yet?'

My old friend and neighbour, Alec, helping with the sheep on Skye.

For fear you think that life on the croft is nothing but idleness and lazing about, I can assure you there are always repairs to be done to the house to keep it wind and water tight.

Having inherited the sheep, we had to find out more about them. They were kept on the hill, which was common grazing land and covered about eighteen hundred acres. This was used by the whole of the township.

When it came to gathering time, for clipping or dipping, the sheep were distinguished by their ear tags and keel markings. The gathering had to be done by a few of the crofters and it never seemed to be convenient for me to be there, so eventually I took our sheep off the hill and put them onto the croft. I also built a dipper and sheep pens so that I could carry out the essential sheep-minding duties to fit in with my holidays. Immodestly, I would point out that despite being an amateur shepherd, I increased the lambing from under a hundred per cent, or one per ewe, to almost two hundred per cent, or twins for every ewe. My secret ingredients were no more than having my own feed shed with hay racks inside.

Our elderly neighbour, Alec, who was also a friend, used to feed the sheep in the winter, but one year he became unwell so I decided to bring them to Balmullo for the winter and lamb them closer to my home.

In the spring when it was time to take them back to Skye, I went

Example of how peats are cut on Skye.

to the farm where they were being kept. I found the farmer, who had had a very late night with friends. In a possible alcoholic haze, he made me a great offer for the sheep but I refused it and we loaded them into my truck and set sail. Unfortunately, the vehicle broke down outside Perth and I had to be towed back to the farm, where I asked the farmer if the offer still stood. By now, he was wide awake and the price dropped to only about half the original bid. I was fed up by this time so I phoned Mairi in Skye and said, 'That is it. No more sheep.' I sold them for almost enough money to put a new gearbox in the truck. But my short sojourn as a shepherd was fun while it lasted.

Another part of Highland and Island life came when we found out we had inherited access to the peat bog. This allowed us to cut peats in the spring time, usually April or May. It was usually a two-man job, but in our case I cut them with the peat iron and Mairi lifted them. There they dried out before being brought home for the winter. The next generation now makes peat cutting a social event with all the family working at it. If I, as overseer, see them slack at their task, I remind them there is nothing better than sitting at a good peat fire in the winter.

Back in Balmullo I am now in my second term as chairman of the local Burns Club, which is now in its thirty-fifth year and our annual Burns supper still commands a full house.

The church has always been high on my list of priorities. I have been an elder for more than forty years, having been inducted at Logie church. When that church closed, Mairi and I moved to St Athernase in Leuchars.

Despite all the parts of my retired life keeping me busy, I still have time to think about how proud my father and his father and all the other Wilson family blacksmiths would have been of my successes.

Similarly, I am quietly proud of the next two generations of blacksmiths. Son David G. Wilson and grandsons Josh and Eli run their business from Balmullo smiddy. Unlike me, who did both blacksmithing and farriery work, their business is solely horseshoeing.

Looking at the mobile gas forges and machine-made horseshoe nails of all sizes, would the past generations of blacksmiths and farriers ever believe this could have happened?

I wonder what the next two hundred years will bring.

Four Wilsons, four blacksmiths. From left: Josh, myself, Eli and David.